500 THINGS
you should know about
SCIENCE

500 THINGS
you should know about
SCIENCE

Clare Oliver
Steve Parker
Peter Riley

Consultants: Clive Carpenter
Peter Riley

Miles Kelly
PUBLISHING

Project Management: Belinda Gallagher
Assistant Editor: Nicola Sail
Designer: John Christopher, White Design
Proofreader: Lynn Bresler
Production: Estela Godoy

British Library Cataloguing-in-Publication Data
A catalogue record for this book is available from the British Library

ISBN 1-84236-365-4

Printed in Singapore

ACKNOWLEDGEMENTS

The publishers would like to thank the following artists who have contributed to this book:

Mark Bergin
Steve Caldwell
Jim Channell
Kuo Kang Chen
Peter Dennis
Richard Draper
Nicholas Forder
Mike Foster/Maltings Partnership
Chris Forsey
Mark Franklin
Terry Gabbey
Studio Galante
Shammi Ghale
Alan Hancocks
Peter Harper
Alan Harris

Kevin Maddison
Alan Male
Janos Marffy
Helen Parsley
Rachel Phillips
Terry Riley
Tony Wilkins
Steve Roberts
Martin Sanders
Peter Sarson
Sarah Smith
Mike Saunders
Gwen Tourret
Rudi Vizi
Steve Weston

Cartoons by Mark Davis at Mackerel

www.mileskelly.net
info@mileskelly.net

Contents

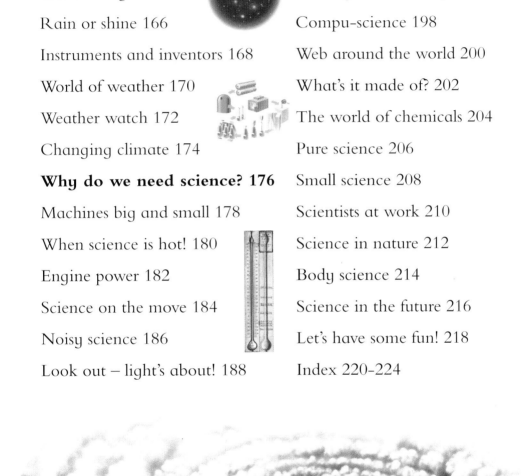

The speedy space ball

1 The Earth is a huge ball of rock moving through space at nearly 3000 metres per second. It weighs 6000 million, million, million tonnes. Up to two-thirds of the Earth's rocky surface is covered by water – this makes the seas and oceans. Rock that is not covered by water makes the land. Surrounding the Earth is a layer of gases called the atmosphere (air). This reaches about 700 kilometres from the Earth's surface – then space begins.

Where did Earth come from?

2 **The Earth came from a cloud in space.** Scientists think the Earth formed from a huge cloud of gas and dust around 4500 million years ago. A star near the cloud exploded, making the cloud spin. As the cloud spun around, gases gathered at its centre and formed the Sun. Dust whizzed around the Sun and stuck together to form lumps of rock. In time the rocks crashed into each other to make the planets. The Earth is one of these planets.

5. The Earth was made up of one large piece of land, now split into seven chunks known as continents

▶ Clouds of gas and dust are made by the remains of old stars that have exploded or simply stopped shining. It is here that new stars and their planets form.

1. Cloud starts to spin

4. Volcanoes erupt, releasing gases, helping to form the first atmosphere

3. The Earth begins to cool and a hard shell forms

2. Dust gathers into lumps of rock which form a small planet

3 **At first the Earth was very hot.** As the rocks crashed together they warmed each other up. Later, as the Earth formed, the rocks inside it melted. The new Earth was a ball of liquid rock with a thin, solid shell.

4 Huge numbers of large rocks called meteorites crashed into the Earth. They made round hollows on the surface. These hollows are called craters. The Moon was hit with rocks at the same time. Look at the Moon with binoculars – you can see the craters that were made long ago.

▶ The Moon was also hit by rocks in space, and these made huge craters, and mountain ranges up to 5000 metres high.

▼ Erupting volcanoes and fierce storms helped form the atmosphere and oceans. These provided energy that was needed for life on Earth to begin.

5 The oceans and seas formed as the Earth cooled down. Volcanoes erupted, letting out steam, gases and rocks from inside the Earth. As the Earth cooled, the steam changed to water droplets and made clouds. As the Earth cooled further, rain fell from the clouds. It rained for millions of years to make the seas and oceans.

I DON'T BELIEVE IT!

Millions of rocks crash into Earth as it speeds through space. Some larger ones may reach the ground as meteorites.

In a spin

6 **The Earth is like a huge spinning top.** It continues to spin because it was formed from a spinning cloud of gas and dust. It does not spin straight up like a top but leans a little to one side. The Earth takes 24 hours to spin around once. We call this period of time a day.

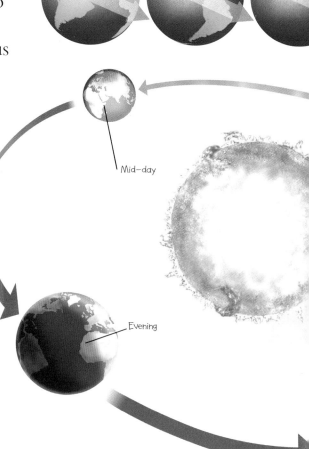

Mid-day

Evening

7 **The Earth's spinning makes day and night.** Each part of the Earth spins towards the Sun, and then away from it every day. When a part of the Earth is facing the Sun it is day-time there. When that part is facing away from the Sun it is night-time. Is the Earth facing the Sun or facing away from it where you are?

◀ If you were in space and looked at the Earth from the side, it would appear to move from left to right. If you looked down on Earth from the North Pole, it would seem to be moving anticlockwise.

8 **The Earth spins around its Poles.** The Earth spins around two points on its surface. They are at opposite ends of the Earth. One is on top of the Earth. It is called the North Pole. The other is at the bottom of the Earth. It is called the South Pole. The North and South Poles are so cold, they are covered by ice and snow.

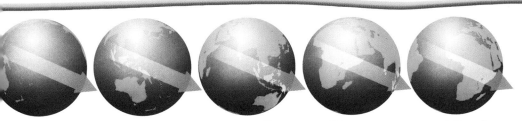

▲ The Earth moves around the Sun in a path called an orbit. It takes a year to make this journey. In that time it spins round 365 and a quarter times.

Morning

Night

▲ As one part of the Earth turns into sunlight, another part turns into darkness. It is morning when a part turns into sunlight, and evening when it turns into darkness.

MAKE A COMPASS

A compass is used to find the direction of the North and South Poles.

You will need:

a bowl of water   a piece of wood
a bar magnet   a real compass

Place the wood in the water with the magnet on top. Make sure they do not touch the sides. When the wood is still, check the direction the magnet is pointing in with your compass, by placing it on a flat surface. It will tell you the direction of the North and South Poles.

9 The spinning Earth acts like a magnet. At the centre of the Earth is liquid iron. As the Earth spins, it makes the iron behave like a magnet with a North and South Pole. These act on the magnet in a compass to make the needle point to the North and South Poles.

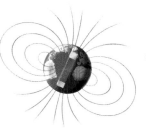

▲ These lines show the pulling power of the magnet inside the Earth.

Inside the Earth

10 **There are different parts to the Earth.** There is a thin, rocky crust, a solid middle called the mantle and a centre called the core. The outer part of the core is liquid but the inner core is made of solid metal.

11 **At the centre of the Earth is a huge metal ball called the inner core.** It is 2500 kilometres wide and is made mainly from iron, with some nickel. The ball has an incredible temperature of 6000°C – hot enough to make the metals melt. They stay solid because other parts of the Earth push down heavily on them.

12 **Around the centre of the Earth flows a hot, liquid layer of iron and nickel.** This layer is the outer core and is about 2200 kilometres thick. As the Earth spins, the metal ball and liquid layer move at different speeds.

▼ If the Earth could be cut open, this is what you would see inside. It has layers inside it like an onion.

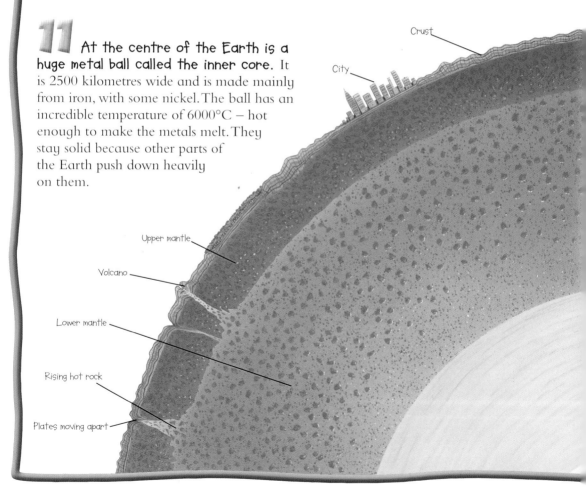

Crust

City

Upper mantle

Volcano

Lower mantle

Rising hot rock

Plates moving apart

13 The largest part of Earth is a layer called the mantle, which is 2900 kilometres thick. It lies between the core and the crust. Near the crust, the mantle is made of slow-moving rock. When you squeeze an open tube of toothpaste, the toothpaste moves a little like the rocks in the upper mantle.

14 The Earth's surface is covered by crust. Land is made of continental crust between 20 and 70 kilometres thick. Most of this is made from a rock called granite. The ocean bed is made of oceanic crust about 8 kilometres thick. It is made mainly from a rock called basalt.

15 The crust is divided into huge slabs of rock called plates. Most plates have land and seas on top of them but some, like the Pacific Plate, are mostly covered by water. The large areas of land on the plates are called continents. There are seven continents – Africa, Asia, Europe, North America, South America, Oceania and Antarctica.

16 Very, very slowly, the continents are moving. Slow-flowing mantle under the crust moves the plates across the Earth's surface. As the plates move, so do the continents. In some places, the plates push into each other. In others, they move apart. North America is moving 3 centimetres away from Europe every year!

Outer core

Inner core

◄ There are gaps in the Earth's crust where hot rocks from inside can reach the surface.

Hot rocks

17 There are places on Earth where hot, liquid rocks shoot up through its surface. These are volcanoes. Beneath a volcano is a huge space filled with molten (liquid) rock. This is the magma chamber. Inside the chamber, pressure builds like the pressure in a fizzy drink's can if you shake it. Ash, steam and molten rock called lava escape from the top of the volcano – this is an eruption.

▲ These volcanoes are a shield volcano (top), a crater volcano (middle) and a cone-shaped volcano (bottom).

18 Volcanoes erupt in different ways and have different shapes. Most have a central tube called a pipe, reaching up to the vent opening. Some volcanoes have runny lava, like those in Hawaii. It flows from the vent and makes a domed shape called a shield volcano. Other volcanoes have thick lava. When they erupt, gases in the lava make it explode into pieces of ash. The ash settles on the lava to make a cone-shaped volcano. A caldera, or crater volcano, is made when the top of a cone-shaped volcano explodes and sinks into the magma chamber.

Cloud of ash, steam and smoke

Layers of rocks from previous eruptions

Lava flowing away from vent

20 Hot rocks don't always reach the surface. Huge lumps of rock rise into the crust and can become stuck. These are batholiths. The rock cools slowly and large crystals form. When the crystals cool, they form a rock called granite. In time, the surface of the crust may wear away and the top of the batholith appears above ground.

◄ When a volcano erupts, the hot rock from inside the Earth escapes as ash, smoke, flying lumps called volcanic bombs and rivers of lava.

Huge chamber of magma (molten rock) beneath the volcano

Molten rock spreading out under the volcano and cooling down

MAKE YOUR OWN VOLCANO
You will need:
bicarbonate of soda   a plastic bottle
food colouring   vinegar   sand
Put a tablespoon of bicarbonate of soda in the plastic bottle. Stand the bottle in a tray and make a cone of sand around it. Put a few drops of red food colouring in half a cup of vinegar. Tip the vinegar into a jug then pour it into the bottle. In a few moments the volcano should erupt with red, frothy lava.

19 There are volcanoes under the sea. Where plates in the crust move apart, lava flows out from rift volcanoes to fill the gap. The hot lava is cooled quickly by the sea and forms pillow-shaped lumps called pillow lava.

Boil and bubble

21 **A geyser can be found on top of some old volcanoes.** If these volcanoes collapse, their rocks settle above hot rocks in the old magma chamber. The gaps between the broken rocks make a group of pipes and chambers. Rainwater seeps in, collecting in the chambers, where it is heated until it boils. Steam builds up, pushing the water through the pipes and out of a cone-shaped opening called a nozzle. Steam and water shoot through the nozzle, making a fountain up to 60 metres high.

▲ Geysers are common in the volcanic regions of New Zealand in Oceania. In some areas they are even used to help make electricity.

22 **In the ocean are hot springs called black smokers.** They form near rift volcanoes, where water is heated by the volcanoes' magma chambers. The hot water dissolves chemicals in the rocks, which turn black when they are cooled by the surrounding ocean water. They rise like clouds of smoke from chimneys.

23 **In a hot spring, the water bubbles gently to the surface.** As the water is heated in the chamber, it rises up a pipe and into a pool. The pool may be brightly coloured due to tiny plants and animals called algae and bacteria. These live in large numbers in the hot water.

◄ The chimneys of a black smoker are made by chemicals in the hot water. These stick together to form a rocky pipe.

24 Wallowing in a mud pot can make your skin soft and smooth. A mud pot is made when fumes break down rocks into tiny pieces. These mix with water to make mud. Hot fumes push through the mud, making it bubble. Some mud pots are cool enough to wallow in.

▼ Mud pot

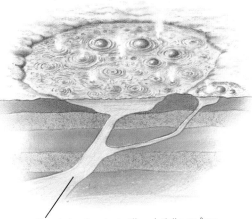

Very hot water mixes with mud at the surface

▲ The bubbles in a mud pot grow as they fill with fumes. Eventually they pop and the fumes escape into the air.

25 Steam and smelly fumes can escape from holes in the ground. These holes are called fumaroles. Since Roman times, people have used the steam from fumaroles for steam baths. The steam may keep joints and lungs healthy.

▼ Fumarole   Released steam

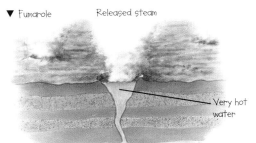

Very hot water

▲ Under a fumarole the water gets so hot that it turns to steam, then shoots upwards into the air.

MAKE A GEYSER
You will need:
a bucket   a plastic funnel
plastic tubing
Fill a bucket with water. Turn the plastic funnel upside down and sink most of it in the water. Take a piece of plastic tube and put one end under the funnel. Blow down the other end of the tube. A spray of water and air will shoot out of the funnel. Be prepared for a wet face!

26 In Iceland, underground steam is used to make lights work. The steam is sent to power stations and is used to work generators to make electricity. The electricity then flows to homes and powers electrical equipment such as lights, televisions and computers.

Breaking down rocks

27 **Ice has the power to make rocks crumble.** In cold weather, rainwater gets into cracks in rocks and freezes. Water swells as it turns to ice. The ice pushes with such power on the rock that it opens up the cracks. Over a long time, a rock can be broken down into thousands of tiny pieces.

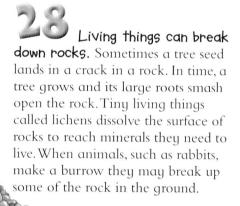
Ice breaking down rock

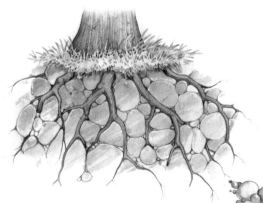
A tree root pushing its way through rock

28 **Living things can break down rocks.** Sometimes a tree seed lands in a crack in a rock. In time, a tree grows and its large roots smash open the rock. Tiny living things called lichens dissolve the surface of rocks to reach minerals they need to live. When animals, such as rabbits, make a burrow they may break up some of the rock in the ground.

29 **Warming up and cooling down can break rocks into flakes.** When a rock warms up it swells a little. When it cools, the rock shrinks back to its original size. After swelling and shrinking many times some rocks break up into flakes. Sometimes layers of large flakes form on a rock and make it look like onion skin.

▶ The flakes of rock break off unevenly and make patterns of ridges on the rock surface.

30 Glaciers break up rocks and carry them away. Glaciers are huge areas of ice which form near mountain tops. They slide slowly down the mountainside and melt. As a glacier moves, some rocks are snapped off and carried along. Others are ground up and carried along as grit and sand.

▶ Snow falls on mountain tops and squashes down to make ice. The ice forms the glacier which slowly moves down the mountainside until it melts.

Region where glacier forms

Moving ice

Where the glacier melts is called the snout

31 Rocks in rivers and seas are always getting smaller. Water flows over rocks, gradually wearing them down. The water also dissolves minerals from the rock. As well as this, sand and grit in the water slowly grind away the rock surfaces.

I DON'T BELIEVE IT!
In one part of Turkey, people have cut caves in huge cones of rock to make homes.

32 Wind can blow a rock to pieces, but it takes a long time. Strong winds hurl dust and sand grains at a rock, which slowly blast pieces from its surface. It then blows away any tiny loose chips that have formed on the surface of the rock.

Smooth rock face

Arch

Settling down

33 Stones of different sizes can stick together to make rock. Thousands of years ago, boulders, pebbles and gravel settled on the shores of seas and lakes. These have become stuck together to make a rock called conglomerate. At the foot of cliffs, broken, rocky pieces collected and stuck together to make a rock called breccia. The lumps in breccia have sharp edges.

▲ Pieces of rock can become stuck together by a natural cement to make a lump of larger rock, such as breccia

34 Sandstone can be made in the sea or in the desert. When a thick layer of sand builds up, the grains are pressed together and cement forms. This sticks the grains together to make sandstone. Sea sandstone may be yellow with sharp-edged grains. Desert sandstone may be red with round, smooth grains.

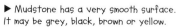

▲ Natural cement binds grains of sand together to make sandstone.

35 If mud is squashed hard enough, it turns to stone. Mud is made from tiny particles of clay and slightly larger particles called silt. When huge layers of mud formed in ancient rivers, lakes and seas, they were squashed by their own weight to make mudstone.

▶ Mudstone has a very smooth surface. It may be grey, black, brown or yellow.

36 Limestone is made from sea shells. Many kinds of sea animal have a hard shell. When the animal dies, the shell remains on the sea floor. In time, large numbers of shells build up and press together to form limestone. Huge numbers of shells become fossils.

▶ Limestone is usually white, cream, grey or yellow. Caves often form in areas of limestone.

SEE BITS OF ROCK SETTLE

You will need:

sand clay gravel a plastic bottle

Put a tablespoon of sand, clay and gravel into a bowl. Mix up the gravel with two cups of water then pour into a plastic bottle. You should see the bits of gravel settle in layers, with the smallest pieces at the bottom and the largest at the top.

37 Chalk is made from millions of shells and the remains of tiny sea creatures. A drop of sea water contains many microscopic organisms (living things). Some of these organisms have shells full of holes. When these organisms die, the shells sink to the sea bed and in time form chalk.

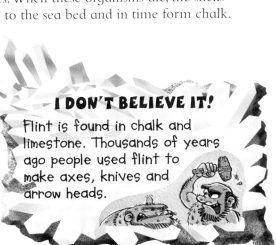

I DON'T BELIEVE IT!

Flint is found in chalk and limestone. Thousands of years ago people used flint to make axes, knives and arrow heads.

▲ Most chalk formed at the time of the dinosaurs, but chalk is forming in some places on the Earth today.

Uncovering fossils

38 **The best fossils formed from animals and plants that were buried quickly.** When a plant or animal dies, it is usually eaten by other living things so that nothing remains. If the plant or animal was buried quickly after death, or even buried alive, its body may be preserved.

39 **A fossil is made from minerals.** A dead plant or animal can be dissolved by water. An empty space in the shape of the plant or animal is left in the mud and fills with minerals from the surrounding rock. Sometimes, the minerals simply settle in the body, making it harder and heavier.

▶ This is a fossil skull of *Tyrannosaurus rex*, a dinosaur that roamed the Earth around 70–65 million years ago.

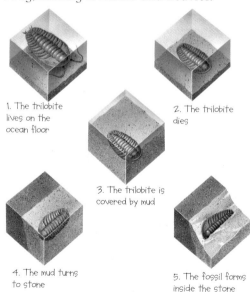

1. The trilobite lives on the ocean floor

2. The trilobite dies

3. The trilobite is covered by mud

4. The mud turns to stone

5. The fossil forms inside the stone

▲ Many fossils of trilobites, small ocean–dwelling creatures, have been found.

40 **Some fossils look like coiled snakes but are really shellfish.** These are ammonites. An ammonite's body was covered by a spiral shell. The body rotted away leaving the shell to become the fossil. Ammonites lived in the seas at the same time as the dinosaurs lived on land.

▲ When this ammonite was alive, tentacles would have stuck out of the uncoiled end of the shell.

41 **Dinosaurs did not just leave fossil bones.** Some left whole skeletons behind while others are known from only a few bones. Fossilized teeth, skin, eggs and droppings have been found. When dinosaurs walked across mud they left tracks behind that became fossils. By looking at these, scientists have discovered how dinosaurs walked and how fast they could run.

42 **Electricity in your home may have been made by burning fossils.** About 300 million years ago the land was covered by forests and swamps. When plants died they fell into the swamps and did not rot away. Over time, their remains were squashed and heated so much that they turned to coal. Today, coal is used to work generators that make electricity.

I DON'T BELIEVE IT!
Some fossils of bacteria are three and a half billion years old.

▶ Coal was formed by trees and plants growing near water. When the trees died the waterlogged ground stopped them rotting away, and peat formed.

Dead trees are buried and squashed to form peat

The peat hardens to form coal

Rocks that change

43 When a rock forms in the crust it may soon be changed again. There are two main ways this can happen. In one way, the rock is heated by hot rocks moving up through the crust. In another way the crust is squashed and heated as mountains form. Both of these ways make crystals in the rock change to form new types of rocks.

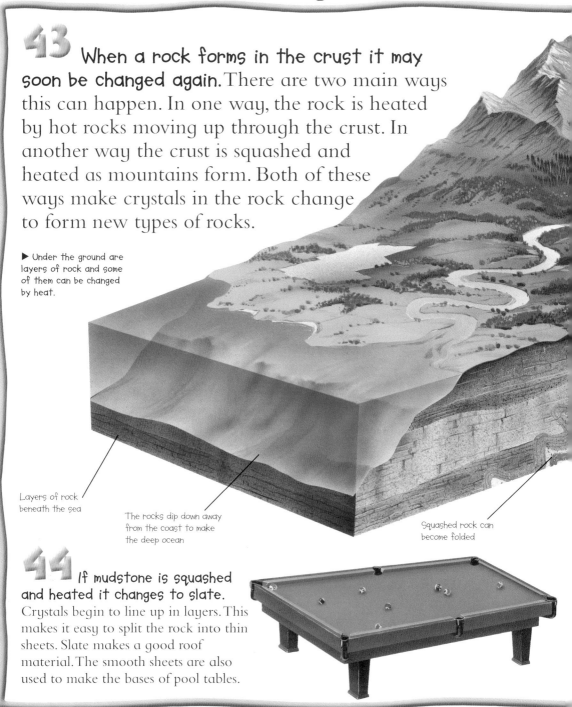

▶ Under the ground are layers of rock and some of them can be changed by heat.

Layers of rock beneath the sea

The rocks dip down away from the coast to make the deep ocean

Squashed rock can become folded

44 If mudstone is squashed and heated it changes to slate. Crystals begin to line up in layers. This makes it easy to split the rock into thin sheets. Slate makes a good roof material. The smooth sheets are also used to make the bases of pool tables.

46 Rock can become stripy when it is heated and folded. It becomes so hot, it almost melts. Minerals that make up the rock form layers that appear as coloured stripes. These stripes may be wavy, showing the way the rock has been folded. This rock is called gneiss (sounds like 'nice').

Some hot rock travels to the surface through the pipe in a volcano

▲ The stripes in gneiss are formed by layers of different minerals.

Layers of rock away from the heat remain unchanged

Hot rock trapped in the crust can change the rock around it

45 If limestone is cooked in the crust it turns to marble. The shells which make up limestone break up when they are heated strongly and form marble, a rock which has a sugary appearance. The surface of marble can be polished to make it look attractive and it is used to make statues and ornaments.

QUIZ
1. If a sandstone has red, round, smooth grains, where was the sand made?
2. Which rocks are made from seashells and tiny sea creatures?
3. Name six kinds of dinosaur fossil.
4. Which rock changes into slate?

Answers:
1. The desert 2. Limestone and chalk
3. Bones, teeth, skin, eggs, droppings, tracks
4. Mudstone

27

Massive mountains

47 The youngest mountains on Earth are the highest. Highest of all is Mount Everest, which formed 15 million years ago. Young mountains have jagged peaks because softer rocks on the mountain top are broken down by the weather. These pointy peaks are made from harder rocks that take longer to break down. In time, even these hard rocks are worn away. This makes an older mountain shorter and gives its top a rounded shape.

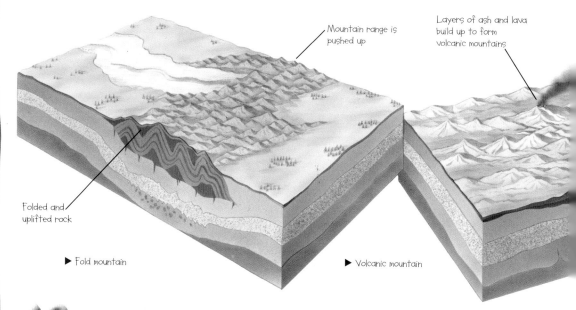

Mountain range is pushed up

Layers of ash and lava build up to form volcanic mountains

Folded and uplifted rock

▶ Fold mountain

▶ Volcanic mountain

48 When plates in the Earth's crust crash together, mountains are formed. When two continental plates crash together, the crust at the edge of the plates crumples and folds, pushing up ranges of mountains. The Himalayan Mountains in Asia formed in this way.

49 Some of the Earth's highest mountains are volcanoes. These are formed when molten rock (lava) erupts through the Earth's crust. As the lava cools, it forms a rocky layer. With each new eruption, another layer is added.

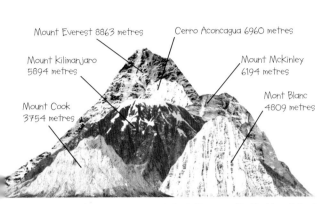

Mount Everest 8863 metres

Cerro Aconcagua 6960 metres

Mount Kilimanjaro 5894 metres

Mount Mckinley 6194 metres

Mont Blanc 4809 metres

Mount Cook 3754 metres

▲ Mountains are the tallest things on Earth. Mount Cook is the smallest mountain shown here, and is still six times taller than the world's tallest man-made structure!

MAKE FOLD MOUNTAINS

Put a towel on a table top. Place one hand at either end of the towel. Push your hands together slowly and watch miniature fold mountains form.

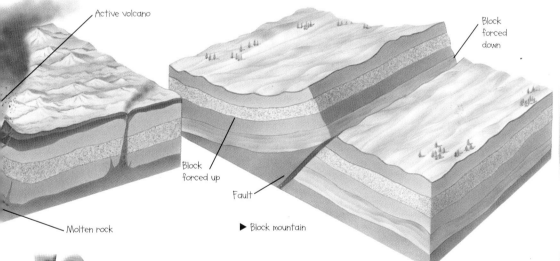

Active volcano

Block forced down

Block forced up

Fault

Molten rock

▶ Block mountain

50 The movement of the Earth's crust can make blocks of rock pop up to make mountains. When the plates in the crust push together, they make heat which softens the rock, letting it fold. Farther away from this heat, cooler rock snaps when it is pushed. The snapped rock makes huge cracks called faults in the crust. When a block of rock between two faults is pushed by the rest of the crust, it rises to form a block mountain.

▲ It takes millions of years for mountains to form and the process is happening all the time. A group of mountains is called a range. The biggest ranges are the Alps in Europe, the Andes in South America, the Rockies in North America and the highest of all – the Himalayas in Asia.

Shaking the Earth

51 **An earthquake is caused by violent movements in the Earth's crust.** Most occur when two plates in the crust rub together. An earthquake starts deep underground at its 'focus'. Shock waves move from the focus in all directions, shaking the rock. Where the shock waves reach the surface is called the epicentre. This is where the greatest shaking occurs.

52 **The power of an earthquake can vary.** Half a million earthquakes happen every year but hardly any can be felt by people. About 25 earthquakes each year are powerful enough to cause disasters. Earthquake strength is measured by the Richter Scale. The higher the number, the more destructive the earthquake.

▼ Earthquakes can make buildings collapse and cause cracks in roads. Fire is also a hazard, as gas mains can break and catch alight.

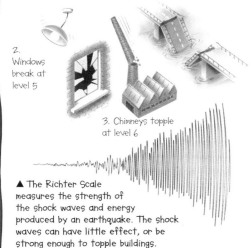

1. Lights swing at level 3

4. Bridges and buildings collapse at level 7

2. Windows break at level 5

3. Chimneys topple at level 6

▲ The Richter Scale measures the strength of the shock waves and energy produced by an earthquake. The shock waves can have little effect, or be strong enough to topple buildings.

Shock waves from the focus.

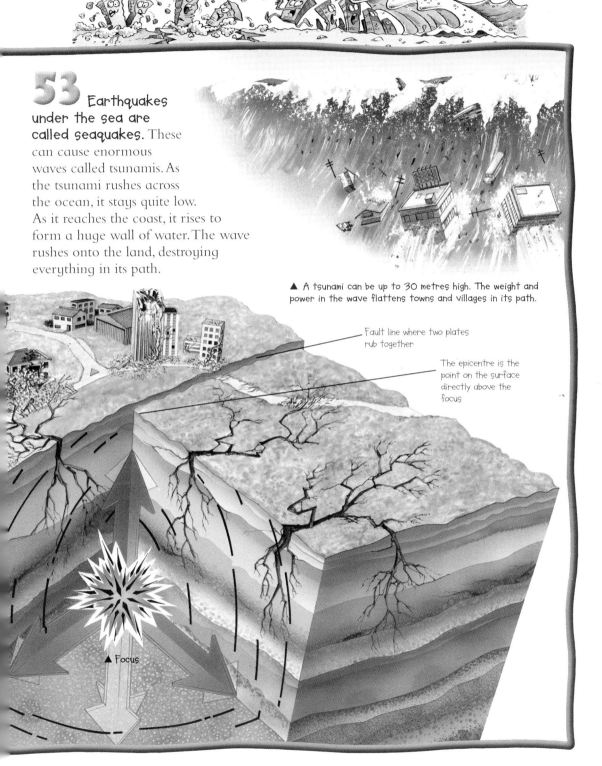

53 **Earthquakes under the sea are called seaquakes.** These can cause enormous waves called tsunamis. As the tsunami rushes across the ocean, it stays quite low. As it reaches the coast, it rises to form a huge wall of water. The wave rushes onto the land, destroying everything in its path.

▲ A tsunami can be up to 30 metres high. The weight and power in the wave flattens towns and villages in its path.

Fault line where two plates rub together

The epicentre is the point on the surface directly above the focus

▲ Focus

Cavernous caves

54 **Some caves are made from a tube of lava.** As lava moves down the side of a volcano, its surface cools down quickly. The cold lava becomes solid but below, the lava remains warm and keeps on flowing. Under the solid surface a tube may form in which liquid lava flows. When the tube empties, a cave is formed.

▲ A cave made by lava is so large that people can walk through it without having to bend down.

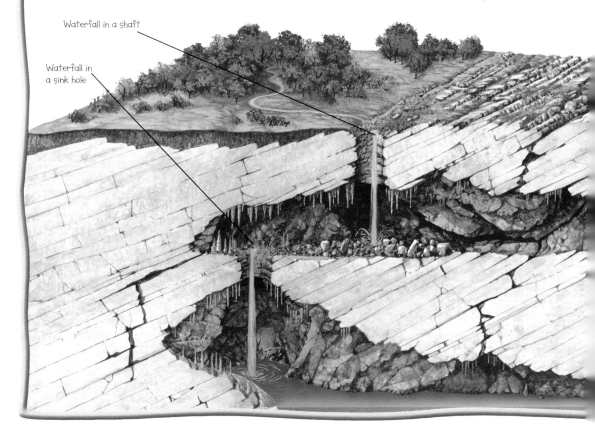

Waterfall in a shaft

Waterfall in a sink hole

1. Water seeps through cracks in rock

55 When rain falls on limestone it becomes a cave-maker. Rainwater can mix with carbon dioxide to form an acid strong enough to attack limestone and make it dissolve. Underground, the action of the rainwater makes caves in which streams and lakes can be found.

▶ Water runs through the caves in limestone rock and makes pools and streams. In wet weather it may flood the caves.

▼ Water flows through the cracks in limestone and makes them wider to form caves. The horizontal caves are called galleries and the vertical caves are called shafts

2. Underground stream carves into rock

3. Large cave system develops

Gallery

Cave opening

I DON'T BELIEVE IT!
The longest stalactite is 59 metres long. The tallest stalagmite is 32 metres tall.

56 Dripping water in a limestone cave makes rock spikes. When water drips from a cave roof it leaves a small piece of limestone behind. A small spike of rock begins to form. This rock spike, called a stalactite, may grow from the ceiling. Where the drops splash onto the cave floor, tiny pieces of limestone gather. They form a spike which points upwards. This is a stalagmite. Over long periods of time, the two spikes may join together to form a column of rock.

The Earth's treasure

57 Gold may form small grains, large nuggets or veins in the rocks. When the rocks wear away, the grains may be found in the sand of river beds. Silver forms branching wires in rock. It does not shine like jewellery but is covered in a black coating called tarnish.

▲ Gold nuggets like this one can be melted and moulded to form all kinds of jewellery.

58 Most metals are found in rocks called ores. An ore is a mixture of different substances, of which metal is one. Each metal has its own ore. For example, aluminium is found in a yellow ore called bauxite. Heat is used to get metals from their ores. We use metals to make thousands of different things, ranging from watches to jumbo jets.

◀ Silver is used for making jewellery and ornaments.

59 Beautiful crystals can grow in lava bubbles. Lava contains gases which form bubbles. When the lava cools and becomes solid, the bubbles form balloon-shaped spaces in the rock. These are called geodes. Liquids seep into them and form large crystals. The gemstone amethyst forms in this way.

▶ Inside a geode there is space for crystals, such as amethyst crystals, to spread out, grow and form perfect shapes.

▲ This is bauxite, the ore of aluminium. Heat, chemicals and electricity are used to get the metal out of the rock. Aluminium is used to make all kinds of things, from kitchen foil to aeroplanes.

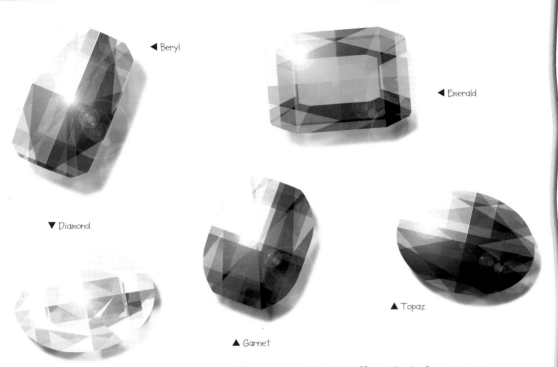

◀ Beryl

◀ Emerald

▼ Diamond

▲ Garnet

▲ Topaz

▲ There are more than 100 different kinds of gemstone. Some are associated with different months of the year and are known as 'birthstones'. For example, the birthstone for September is sapphire.

60 Gemstones are coloured rocks which are cut and polished to make them sparkle. People have used them to make jewellery for thousands of years. Gems such as topaz, emerald and garnet formed in hot rocks which rose to the Earth's crust and cooled. Most are found as small crystals, but a gem called beryl can have a huge crystal – the largest ever found was 18 metres long! Diamond is a gemstone and is the hardest natural substance found on Earth.

MAKE CRYSTALS FROM SALT WATER

You will need:

table salt
a magnifying glass
a dark-coloured bowl

Dissolve some table salt in some warm water. Pour the salty water into a dark-coloured bowl. Put the bowl in a warm place so the water can evaporate. After a few days, you can look at the crystals with a magnifying glass.

Wild weather

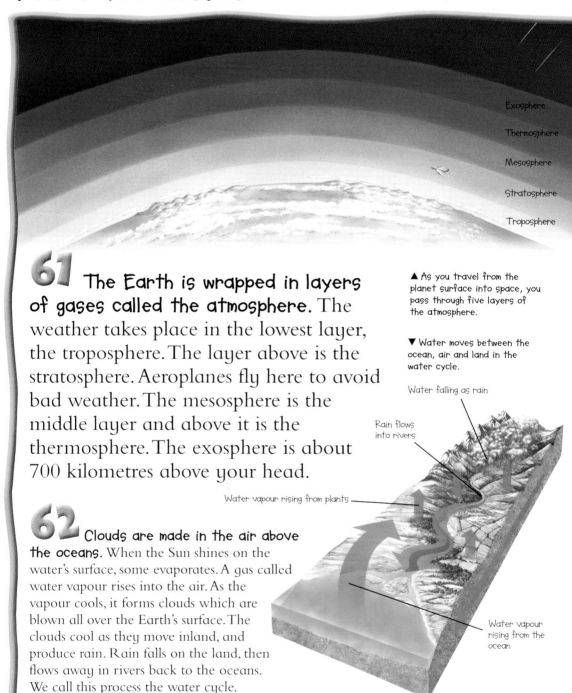

Exosphere

Thermosphere

Mesosphere

Stratosphere

Troposphere

61 **The Earth is wrapped in layers of gases called the atmosphere.** The weather takes place in the lowest layer, the troposphere. The layer above is the stratosphere. Aeroplanes fly here to avoid bad weather. The mesosphere is the middle layer and above it is the thermosphere. The exosphere is about 700 kilometres above your head.

▲ As you travel from the planet surface into space, you pass through five layers of the atmosphere.

▼ Water moves between the ocean, air and land in the water cycle.

Water falling as rain

Rain flows into rivers

Water vapour rising from plants

Water vapour rising from the ocean

62 Clouds are made in the air above the oceans. When the Sun shines on the water's surface, some evaporates. A gas called water vapour rises into the air. As the vapour cools, it forms clouds which are blown all over the Earth's surface. The clouds cool as they move inland, and produce rain. Rain falls on the land, then flows away in rivers back to the oceans. We call this process the water cycle.

▶ A hurricane forms over the surface of a warm ocean but it can move to the coast and onto the land.

63 A hurricane is a destructive storm which gathers over a warm part of the ocean. Water evaporating from the ocean forms a vast cloud. As cool air rushes in below the cloud, it turns like a huge spinning wheel. The centre of the hurricane (the eye) is completely still. But all around, winds gust at speeds of 300 kilometres an hour. If it reaches land the hurricane can blow buildings to pieces.

65 Snowflakes form in the tops of clouds. It is so cold here that water freezes to make ice crystals. As the snowflakes get larger, they fall through the cloud. If the cloud is in warm air, the snowflakes melt and form raindrops. If the cloud is in cold air, the snowflakes reach the ground and begin to settle.

▼ The ice crystals in a snowflake usually form six arms.

64 A tornado is the fastest wind on Earth – it can spin at speeds of 500 kilometres an hour. Tornadoes form over ground that has become very warm. Fast-rising air makes a spinning funnel which acts as a vacuum cleaner. It can devastate buildings and lift up cars and traffic, flinging them to the ground.

I DON'T BELIEVE IT!
Every day there are 45,000 thunderstorms on the Earth.

Lands of sand and grass

66 The driest places on Earth are deserts. In many deserts there is a short period of rain every year, but some deserts have dry weather for many years. The main deserts of the world are shown on the map.

▲ 1. North American deserts – Great Basin and Mojave 2. Atacama 3. Sahara 4. Arabian 5. Gobi 6. Australian deserts – Great Sandy, Gibson, Great Victoria, Simpson.

67 Deserts are not always hot. It can be as hot as 50°C in the day-time but at night the temperature falls quickly. Deserts near the Equator have hot days all year round but some deserts farther from the Equator have very cold winters.

Ridges of sand being blown into dunes

Barchan dune

Rock beneath the desert

I DON'T BELIEVE IT!
The camel has broad feet that stop it sinking in the sand.

68 Sand dunes are made by the winds blowing across a desert. If there is only a small amount of sand on the desert floor, the wind blows crescent-shaped dunes called barchans. If there is plenty of sand, it forms long, straight dunes called transverse dunes. If the wind blows in two directions, it makes long wavy dunes called seif dunes.

69 An oasis is a pool of water in the desert. It forms from rainwater that has seeped into the sand then collected in rock. The water then moves through the rock to where the sand is very thin and forms a pool. Trees and plants grow around the pool and animals visit the pool to drink.

▼ Plants and animals can thrive at an oasis in the middle of a desert.

Oasis

70 A desert cactus stores water in its stem. The grooves on the stem let it swell with water to keep the plant alive in dry weather. The spines stop animals biting into the cactus for a drink.

71 Grasslands are found where there is too much rain for a desert and not enough rain for a forest. Tropical grasslands near the Equator are hot all year round. Grasslands farther from the Equator have warm summers and cool winters.

72 Large numbers of animals live on grasslands. In Africa zebras feed on the top of grass stalks, gnu feed on the middle leaves and gazelles feed on the new shoots. This allows all the animals to feed together. Other animals such as lions feed on plant eaters.

▼ Three types of animals can live together by eating plants of different heights. Zebras (1) eat the tall grass. Gnu (2) eat the middle shoots and gazelle (3) browse on the lowest shoots.

1

2

3

Fantastic forests

73 **There are three main kinds of forest.** They are coniferous, temperate and tropical forests. The main forest regions are shown on the world map opposite.

▲ This map shows the major areas of forest in the world.
1. Coniferous forest 2. Temperate forest
3. Tropical forest

74 **Coniferous trees form huge forests around the northern part of the planet.** They have long, green, needle-like leaves covered in wax. These trees stay in leaf throughout the year. In winter, the wax helps snow slide off the leaves so that sunlight can reach them to keep them alive. Coniferous trees produce seeds in cones. These are eaten by squirrels.

76 Large numbers of huge trees grow close together in a rainforest. They have broad, evergreen leaves and branches that almost touch. These form a leafy roof over the forest called a canopy. It rains almost every day in a rainforest and the vegetation is so thick, it can take a raindrop ten minutes to fall to the ground. Three-quarters of all known species of animals and plants live in rainforests. They include huge hairy spiders, brightly coloured frogs and spotted jungle cats.

75 Most trees in temperate forests have flat, broad leaves and need large amounts of water to keep them alive. In winter, the trees cannot get enough water from the frozen ground, so they lose their leaves and grow new ones in spring. Deer, rabbits, foxes and mice live on the woodland floor while squirrels, woodpeckers and owls live in the trees.

QUIZ

1. What forms at the top of a cloud?
2. What shape is a barchan sand dune?
3. In which kind of forest would you find brightly coloured frogs?

Answers:
1. Snow flake 2. Crescent 3. Tropical

Rivers and lakes

77 **A mighty river can start from a spring.** This is a place where water flows from the ground. Rain soaks into the ground, through the soil and rock, until it gushes out on the side of a hill. The trickle of water from a spring is called a stream. Many streams join together to make a river.

78 **Water wears rocks down to make a waterfall.** When a river flows off a layer of hard rock onto softer rock, it wears the softer rock away. The rocks and pebbles in the water grind the soft rock away to make a cliff face. At the bottom of the waterfall they make a deep pool called a plunge pool.

▼ Waterfalls may only be a few centimetres high, or come crashing over a cliff with a massive drop. Angel Falls in Venezuela form the highest falls in the world. One of the drops is an amazing 807 metres.

Oxbow lake

Meander

Delta

► High in the mountains, streams join to form the headwater of a river. From here the river flows through the mountains then more slowly across the plains to the sea.

79 **A river changes as it flows to the sea.** Rivers begin in hills and mountains. They are narrow and flow quickly there. When the river flows through flatter land it becomes wider and slow-moving. It makes loops called meanders which may separate and form oxbow lakes. Where the river meets the sea is the river mouth. It may be a wide channel called an estuary or a group of sandy islands called a delta.

Headwater

80
Lakes form in hollows in the ground. The hollows may be left when glaciers melt or when plates in the crust split open. Some lakes form when a landslide makes a dam across a river.

▲ A landslide has fallen into the river and blocked the flow of water to make a lake.

▼ A volcano can sometimes form in a lake inside a crater.

81
A lake can form in the crater of a volcano. A few crater lakes have formed in craters left by meteorites that hit Earth long ago.

▼ Most lakes are just blue but some are green, pink, red or even white. The Laguna Colorado in Chile is red due to tiny organisms (creatures) that live in the water.

82
Some lake water may be brightly coloured. The colours are made by tiny organisms called algae or by minerals dissolved in the water.

Water world

83 There is so much water on our planet that it could be called 'Ocean' instead of Earth. Only about one third of the planet is covered by land. The rest is covered by four huge areas of water called oceans. A sea is a smaller area of water in an ocean. For example the North Sea is part of the Atlantic Ocean and the Malayan Sea is part of the Pacific Ocean.

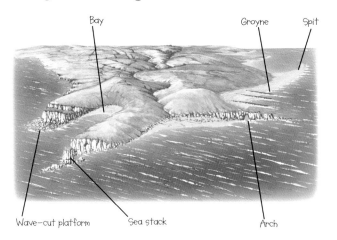

Bay

Groyne

Spit

Wave–cut platform

Sea stack

Arch

84 Coasts are always changing. Where the sea and land meet is called the coast. In many places waves crash onto the land and break it up. Caves and arches are punched into cliffs. In time, the arches break and leave columns of rock called sea stacks.

◀ The rocks at the coast are broken up by the action of the waves.

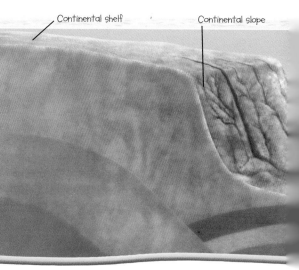

Continental shelf

Continental slope

85 The oceans are so deep that mountains are hidden beneath them. If you paddle by the shore, sea water is quite shallow. Out in the ocean it can be up to 8 kilometres deep. The ocean floor is a flat plain with mountain ranges rising across it. They mark where two places in the crust meet. Nearer the coast may be deep trenches where the edges of two plates have moved apart. Extinct volcanoes form mountains called sea mounts.

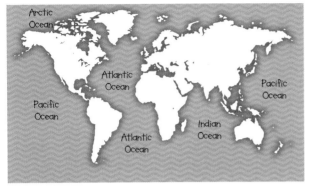

▲ This map shows the major oceans of the world.

87 There are thousands of icebergs floating in the oceans. They are made from glaciers and ice sheets which have formed at the North and South Poles. Only about a tenth of an iceberg can be seen above water. The rest lies below and can sink ships that sail too close.

▲ Under every iceberg is a huge amount of ice, usually much bigger than the area visible from the surface.

86 Tiny creatures can make islands in the oceans. Coral have jelly-like bodies but they live together in their millions. They make rocky homes from minerals in sea water which protects them from feeding fish. Coral builds up to create islands around extinct volcanoes in the Pacific and Indian Oceans.

▲ Corals only grow in tropical or sub-tropical waters. They tend to grow in shallow water where there is lots of sunlight.

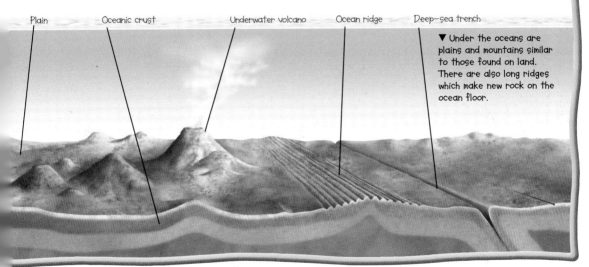

Plain   Oceanic crust   Underwater volcano   Ocean ridge   Deep-sea trench

▼ Under the oceans are plains and mountains similar to those found on land. There are also long ridges which make new rock on the ocean floor.

The planet of life

88 **There are millions of different kinds of life forms on Earth.** So far, life has not been found anywhere else. Living things survive here because it is warm, there is water and the air contains oxygen. If we discover other planets with these conditions, there may be life on them too.

89 **Many living things on the Earth are tiny.** They are so small that we cannot see them. A whale shark is the largest fish on the planet, yet it feeds on tiny shrimp-like creatures. These in turn feed on even smaller plant-like organisms called plankton, which make food from sunlight and sea water. Microscopic bacteria are found in the soil and even on your skin.

▲ Despite being the biggest fish in the oceans, the mighty whale shark feeds on tiny shrimp-like creatures and plankton (right).

90 **Animals cannot live without plants.** A plant makes food from sunlight, water, air and minerals in the soil. Animals cannot make their own food so many of them eat plants. Others survive by eating the plant-eaters. If plants died out, all the animals would die too.

◄ This caterpillar eats as much plant-life as possible before beginning its change to a butterfly.

91 The air can be full of animals. On a warm day, midges and gnats form clouds close to the ground. In spring and autumn flocks of birds fly to different parts of the world to nest. On summer evenings bats hunt for midges flying in the air.

92 The surface of the ground is home to many small animals. Mice scurry through the grass. Larger animals such as deer hide in bushes. The elephant is the largest land animal. It does not need to hide because few animals would attack it.

93 If you dig into the ground you can find animals living there. The earthworm is a common creature found in the soil. It feeds on rotting plants that it pulls into the soil. Earthworms are eaten by moles that dig their way underground.

I DON'T BELIEVE IT!
The star-nosed mole has feelers on the end of its nose. It uses them to find food.

Caring for the planet

94 **Many useful materials come from the Earth.** These make clothes, buildings, furniture and containers such as cans. Some materials, like those used to make buildings, last a long time. Others, such as those used to make cans, may be used up on the day they are bought.

95 **We may run out of some materials in the future.** Metals are found in rocks called ores. When all the ore has been used up we will not be able to make new metal. Wood is a material that we may not run out of as new trees are always being planted. We must still be careful not to use too much wood, because new trees may not grow fast enough for our needs.

1. Old bottles are collected from bottle banks

2. The glass or plastic are recycled to make raw materials

3. The raw materials are re-used to make new bottles

Exhaust fumes from traffic clog up the atmosphere

▲ The waste collected at a recycling centre is changed back into useful materials to make many of the things we frequently use.

96 **We can make materials last longer by recycling them.** Metal, glass and plastic are thrown away after they have been used, buried in tips and never used again. Today more people recycle materials. This means sending them back to factories to be used again.

Factories pump out chemicals that can cause acid rain. They also dump polluted water in rivers and seas.

▼ Here are some of the ways in which we are harming our planet today. We must think of better ways to treat the Earth in the future.

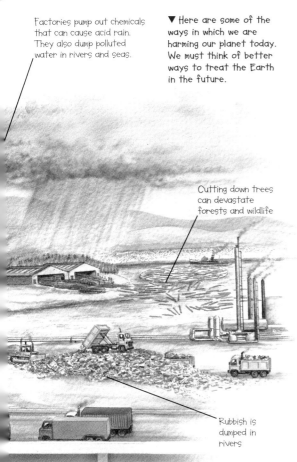

Cutting down trees can devastate forests and wildlife

Rubbish is dumped in rivers

98 **Air and water can be polluted by our activities.** Burning coal and oil makes fumes which can make rainwater acidic. This can kill trees and damages soil. When we make materials, chemicals are often released into rivers and seas, endangering wildlife.

99 **Living things can be protected.** Large areas of land have been made into national parks where wildlife is protected. People can come to study both plants and animals.

100 **The Earth is nearly five billion years old.** From a ball of molten rock it has changed into a living, breathing planet. We must try to keep it that way. Switching off lights to save energy and picking up litter are small things we can all do.

97 **We use huge amounts of fuel to make energy.** The main fuels are coal and oil, which are used in power stations to make electricity. Oil is also used in petrol for cars. In time, these fuels will run out. Scientists are trying to develop ways of using other energy sources such as the wind and wave power. Huge windmills are already used to make electricity.

I DON'T BELIEVE IT!
30 to 50 percent of all living species may be extinct by the middle of the 21st century.

Surrounded by space

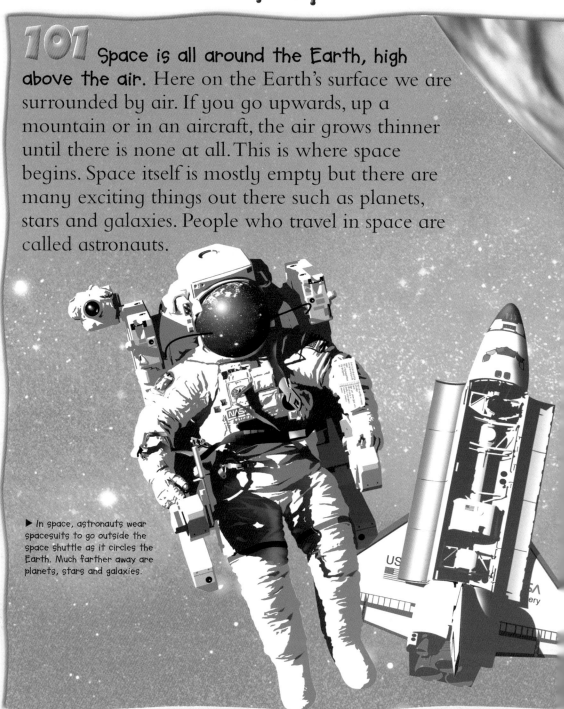

101 **Space is all around the Earth, high above the air.** Here on the Earth's surface we are surrounded by air. If you go upwards, up a mountain or in an aircraft, the air grows thinner until there is none at all. This is where space begins. Space itself is mostly empty but there are many exciting things out there such as planets, stars and galaxies. People who travel in space are called astronauts.

▶ In space, astronauts wear spacesuits to go outside the space shuttle as it circles the Earth. Much farther away are planets, stars and galaxies.

Our life-giving star

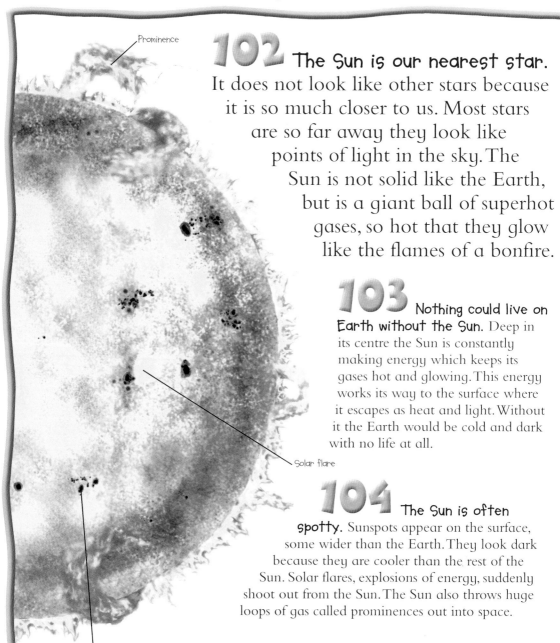

Prominence

102 The Sun is our nearest star. It does not look like other stars because it is so much closer to us. Most stars are so far away they look like points of light in the sky. The Sun is not solid like the Earth, but is a giant ball of superhot gases, so hot that they glow like the flames of a bonfire.

103 Nothing could live on Earth without the Sun. Deep in its centre the Sun is constantly making energy which keeps its gases hot and glowing. This energy works its way to the surface where it escapes as heat and light. Without it the Earth would be cold and dark with no life at all.

Solar flare

104 The Sun is often spotty. Sunspots appear on the surface, some wider than the Earth. They look dark because they are cooler than the rest of the Sun. Solar flares, explosions of energy, suddenly shoot out from the Sun. The Sun also throws huge loops of gas called prominences out into space.

Sunspot

◀ The Sun's hot, glowing gas is always on the move, bubbling up to the surface and sinking back down again.

105 When the Moon hides the Sun there is an eclipse. Every so often, the Sun, Moon and Earth line up in space so that the Moon comes directly between the Earth and the Sun. This stops sunlight from reaching a small area on Earth. This area grows dark and cold, as if night has come early.

▼ When the Moon casts a shadow on the Earth, there is an eclipse of the Sun.

▶ When there is an eclipse, we can see the corona (glowing gas) around the Sun.

Sun

Moon

Shadow of eclipse

I DON'T BELIEVE IT!

The surface of the Sun is nearly 60 times hotter than boiling water. It is so hot it would melt a spacecraft flying near it.

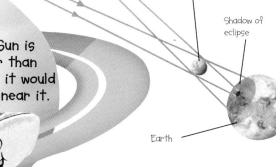

Earth

A family of planets

106 **The Sun is surrounded by a family of circling planets called the Solar System.** This family is held together by an invisible force called gravity, which pulls things towards each other. It is the same force that pulls us to the ground and stops us floating away. The Sun's gravity pulls on the planets and keeps them circling around it.

107 **The Earth is one of nine planets in the Sun's family.** They all circle the Sun at different distances from it. The four planets nearest to the Sun are all balls of rock. The next four planets are much bigger and are made of gas and liquid. The tiny planet at the edge of the Solar System, Pluto, is a solid, icy ball.

108 **Moons circle the planets, travelling with them round the Sun.** Earth has one Moon. It circles the Earth while the Earth circles round the Sun. Pluto also has one moon. Mars has two tiny moons but Mercury and Venus have none. There are large families of moons, like miniature solar systems, around all the large gas planets.

Saturn

Uranus

Neptune

Pluto

Jupiter

Moon

Mercury

Earth

Venus

Mars

Sun

▲ The nine planets are all different. Mercury, nearest the Sun, is small and hot. Then Venus, Earth and Mars are rocky and cooler. Beyond them Jupiter, Saturn, Uranus and Neptune are large and cold, while Pluto is tiny and icy.

109 There are millions of smaller members in the Sun's family. Some are tiny specks of dust speeding through space between the planets. Larger chunks of rock, many as large as mountains, are called asteroids. Comets come from the edge of the Solar System, skimming past the Sun before disappearing.

I DON'T BELIEVE IT !

If the Sun was the size of a large beach ball, the Earth would be as small as a pea, and the Moon would look like a pinhead.

The living planet

110 **The planet we live on is the Earth.** It is a round ball of rock. On the outside where we live the rock is hard and solid. But deep below our feet, inside the Earth, the rock is hot enough to melt. You can sometimes see this hot rock showering out of an erupting volcano.

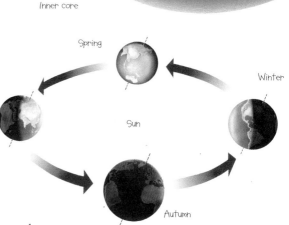

Outer core

Inner core

111 **The Earth is the only planet with living creatures.** From space the Earth is a blue and white planet, with huge oceans and wet masses of cloud. People, animals and plants can live on Earth because of all this water.

Spring

Winter

Summer

Sun

Autumn

112 **Sunshine gives us daylight when it is night on the other side of the Earth.** When it is daytime, your part of the Earth faces towards the Sun and it is light. At night, your part faces away from the Sun and it is dark. Day follows night because the Earth is always turning.

▲ The Earth tilts, so we have different seasons as the Earth moves around the Sun. These are the seasons for the northern half of the Earth.

◀ The inner core at the centre of the Earth is made of iron. It is very hot and keeps the outer core as liquid. Outside this is the mantle, made of thick rock. The thin surface layer that we live on is called the crust.

Crust

Mantle

New Moon

Crescent Moon

First quarter Moon

Gibbous Moon

Full Moon

113 Look for the Moon on clear nights and watch how it seems to change shape. Over a month it changes from a thin crescent to a round shape. This is because sunlight is reflected by the Moon. We see the full Moon when the sunlit side faces the Earth and a thin, crescent shape when the sunlit side is facing away from us.

114 Craters on the Moon are scars from space rocks crashing into the surface. When a rock smashes into the Moon at high speed, it leaves a saucer-shaped dent, pushing some of the rock outwards into a ring of mountains.

The Earth's neighbours

115 Venus and Mars are the nearest planets to the Earth. Venus is closer to the Sun than the Earth while Mars is farther away. Each takes a different amount of time to circle the Sun and we call this its year. A year on Venus is 225 days, on Earth 365 days and on Mars 687 days.

▲ All we can see of Venus from space are the tops of its clouds. They take just four days to race right around the planet.

116 Venus is the hottest planet. It is hotter than Mercury, although Mercury is closer to the Sun and gets more of the Sun's heat. Heat builds up on Venus because it is completely covered by clouds which trap the heat, like the glass in a greenhouse.

117 Venus has poisonous clouds with drops of acid that would burn your skin. They are not like clouds on Earth, which are made of droplets of water. These thick clouds do not let much sunshine reach the surface of Venus.

▼ Under its clouds, Venus has hundreds of volcanoes, large and small, all over its surface. We do not know if any of them are still erupting.

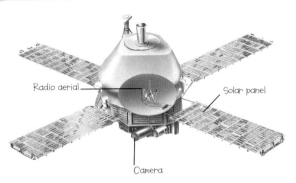

Radio aerial

Solar panel

Camera

119

Winds on Mars whip up huge dust storms that can cover the whole planet. Mars is very dry, like a desert, and covered in red dust. When a space probe called *Mariner 9* arrived there in 1971, the whole planet was hidden by dust clouds.

◀ *Mariner 9* was the first space probe to circle another planet. It sent back over 7000 pictures of Mars showing giant volcanoes, valleys, ice caps and dried-up river beds.

118

Mars has the largest volcano in the Solar System. It is called Olympus Mons and is three times as high as Mount Everest, the tallest mountain on Earth. Olympus Mons is an old volcano and it has not erupted for millions of years.

PLANET-SPOTTING
See if you can spot Venus in the night sky. It is often the first bright 'star' to appear in the evening, just above where the Sun has set. Because of this we sometimes call it the 'evening star'.

120

There are plans to send astronauts to Mars but the journey would take six months or more. The astronauts would have to take with them everything they need for the journey there and back and for their stay on Mars.

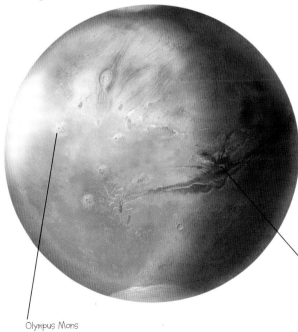

Valles Marineris

Olympus Mons

◀ An enormous valley seems to cut Mars in half. It is called Valles Marineris. To the left is a row of three huge volcanoes and beyond them you can see the largest volcano, Olympus Mons.

The smallest of all

121 **Pluto is the smallest planet.**
It is less that half the width of the next
smallest planet, Mercury. In fact it is
smaller than our Moon. It is so small
and far away that it was not
discovered until 1930.

▲ Pluto is too far away to see any
detail on its surface, but it might
look like this.

122 **Pluto is the farthest
planet from the Sun.** If you were to
stand on its surface, the Sun would not
look much brighter than the other stars.
It gets very little heat from the Sun and its
surface is completely covered with solid ice.

123 **Space probes have visited
every planet except Pluto.** So
astronomers will have to wait for close-up
pictures and detailed information that a
probe could send back. Even if one was
sent to Pluto it would take at least eight
years to get there.

124 **No one knew Pluto had a
moon until 1978.** An astronomer noticed
what looked like a bulge on the side of the
planet. It turned out to be a moon and
was named Charon. Charon is about half
the width of Pluto.

▼ If you were on Pluto, its moon Charon would
look much larger than our Moon does, because
Charon is very close to Pluto.

125

Mercury looks like our Moon. It is a round, cratered ball of rock. Although a little larger than the Moon, like the Moon it has no air.

MAKE CRATERS
You will need:
flour   baking tray
a marble or a stone

Spread some flour about 2 centimetres deep in a baking tray and smooth over the surface. Drop a marble or a small round stone onto the flour and see the saucer-shaped crater that it makes.

◄ Mercury's many craters show how often it was hit by space rocks. One was so large that it shattered rocks on the other side of the planet.

▼ The Sun looks huge as it rises on Mercury. A traveller to Mercury would have to keep out of its heat.

126

The sunny side of Mercury is boiling hot but the night side is freezing cold. Being the nearest planet to the Sun the sunny side can get twice as hot as an oven. But Mercury spins round slowly so the night side has time to cool down, and there is no air to trap the heat. The night side becomes more than twice as cold as the coldest place on Earth – Antarctica.

The biggest of all

127 Jupiter is the biggest planet, more massive than all the other planets in the Solar System put together. It is 11 times as wide as the Earth although it is still much smaller than the Sun. Saturn, the next largest planet, is more than nine times as wide as the Earth.

128 Jupiter and Saturn are gas giants. They have no solid surface for a spacecraft to land on. All that you can see are the tops of their clouds. Beneath the clouds, the planets are made mostly of gas (like air) and liquid (water is a liquid).

▼ Jupiter's fast winds blow the clouds into coloured bands around the planet.

129 The Great Red Spot on Jupiter is a 300-year old storm. It was first noticed about 300 years ago and is at least twice as wide as the Earth. It rises above the rest of the clouds and swirls around like storm clouds on Earth.

▼ There are many storms on Jupiter but none as large or long lasting as the Great Red Spot.

▼ Jupiter's Moon Io is always changing because its many volcanoes throw out new material from deep inside it.

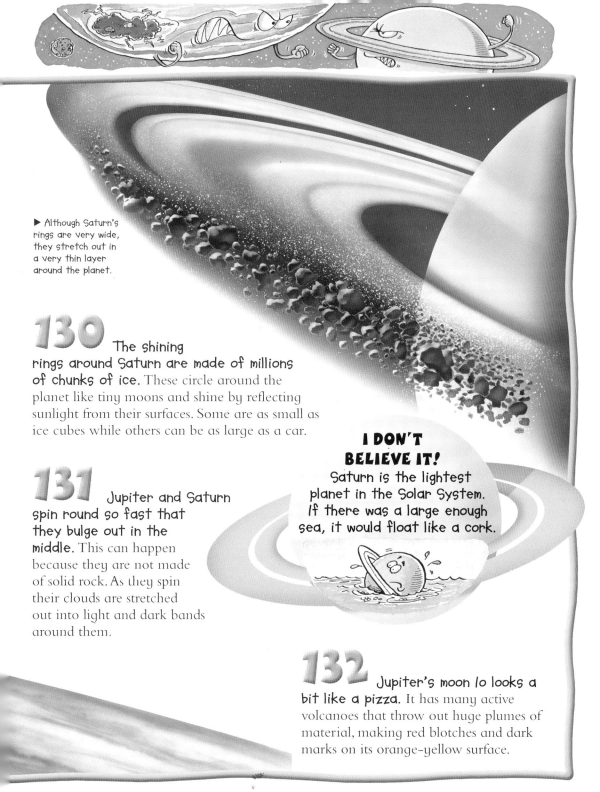

▶ Although Saturn's rings are very wide, they stretch out in a very thin layer around the planet.

130
The shining rings around Saturn are made of millions of chunks of ice. These circle around the planet like tiny moons and shine by reflecting sunlight from their surfaces. Some are as small as ice cubes while others can be as large as a car.

131
Jupiter and Saturn spin round so fast that they bulge out in the middle. This can happen because they are not made of solid rock. As they spin their clouds are stretched out into light and dark bands around them.

I DON'T BELIEVE IT!
Saturn is the lightest planet in the Solar System. If there was a large enough sea, it would float like a cork.

132
Jupiter's moon Io looks a bit like a pizza. It has many active volcanoes that throw out huge plumes of material, making red blotches and dark marks on its orange-yellow surface.

So far away

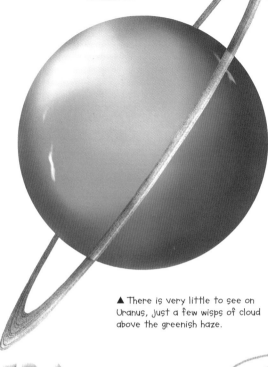

▲ There is very little to see on Uranus, just a few wisps of cloud above the greenish haze.

133 Uranus and Neptune are gas giants like Jupiter and Saturn. They are the next two planets beyond Saturn but much smaller, being less than half as wide. They too have no hard surface. Their cloud tops make Uranus and Neptune both look blue. They are very cold, being so far from the Sun.

134 Uranus seems to 'roll' around the Sun. Unlike most of the other planets, which spin upright, Uranus spins on its side. It may have been knocked over when something crashed into it millions of years ago.

135 Uranus has more moons than any other planet. Twenty-one have been discovered so far, although one is so newly discovered it has not got a name yet. Most are very small but there are five larger ones.

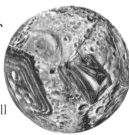

◀ Miranda is one of Uranus' moons. It looks as though it has been split apart and put back together again.

136 **Neptune had a storm that disappeared.** When the *Voyager 2* space probe flew past Neptune in 1989 it spotted a huge storm like a dark version of the Great Red Spot on Jupiter. When the Hubble Space Telescope looked at Neptune in 1994, the storm had gone.

137 **Neptune has bright blue clouds that make the whole planet look blue.** Above these clouds are smaller white streaks. These are icy clouds that race around the planet. One of the white clouds seen by the *Voyager 2* space probe was called 'Scooter' because it scooted around the planet so fast.

138 **Neptune is sometimes farther from the Sun than Pluto.** All the planets travel around the Sun on orbits (paths) that look like circles, but Pluto's path is more squashed. This sometimes brings it closer to the Sun than Neptune.

▼ In the past, astronomers thought there might be another planet, called Planet X, outside Neptune and Pluto.

Orbit of Pluto

Orbit of Planet X

Orbit of Neptune

◄ Like all the gas giant planets, Neptune has rings although they are much darker and thinner than Saturn's rings.

QUIZ
1. How many moons does Uranus have?
2. Which is the biggest planet in our Solar System?
3. Which planet seems to 'roll' around the Sun?
4. What colour are Neptune's clouds?

Answers:
1. 21 2. Jupiter
3. Uranus 4. blue

Comets, asteroids and meteors

139 There are probably billions of tiny comets at the edge of the Solar System. They circle the Sun far beyond the farthest planet, Pluto. Sometimes one is disturbed and moves inwards towards the Sun, looping around it before going back to where it came from. Some comets come back to the Sun regularly, such as Halley's comet that returns every 76 years.

▲ The solid part of a comet is hidden inside a huge, glowing cloud that stretches into a long tail.

140 A comet is often called a dirty snowball because it is made of dust and ice mixed together. Heat from the Sun melts some of the ice. This makes dust and gas stream away from the comet, forming a huge tail that glows in the sunlight.

141 Comet tails always point away from the Sun. Although it looks bright, a comet's tail is extremely thin so it is blown outwards, away from the Sun. When the comet moves away from the Sun, its tail goes in front of it.

143 Asteroids are chunks of rock that failed to stick together to make a planet. Most of them circle the Sun between Mars and Jupiter where there would be room for another planet. There are millions of asteroids, some the size of a car, and others as big as mountains

▶ Asteroids travel in a ring around the Sun. This ring is called the Asteroid belt and can be found between Mars and Jupiter.

142 Meteors are sometimes called shooting stars. They are not really stars, just streaks of light that flash across the night sky. Meteors are made when pebbles racing through space at high speed hit the top of the air above the Earth. The pebble gets so hot it burns up. We see it as a glowing streak for a few seconds.

QUIZ
1. Which way does a comet tail always point?
2. What is another name for a meteor?
3. Where is the asteroid belt?

Answers:
1. Away from the Sun
2. Shooting star
3. Between Mars and Jupiter

▼ At certain times of year there are meteor showers when you can see more shooting stars than usual.

A star is born

144 **Stars are born in clouds of dust and gas in space called nebulae.** Astronomers can see these clouds as shining patches in the night sky, or dark patches against the distant stars. These clouds shrink as gravity pulls the dust and gas together. At the centre, the gas gets hotter and hotter until a new star is born.

1. Clumps of gas in this nebula start to shrink into the tight round balls that will become stars.

2. The gas spirals round as it is pulled inwards. Any left over gas and dust may form planets around the new star.

3. Deep in its centre, the new star starts making energy, but it is still hidden by the cloud of dust and gas.

4. The dust and gas are blown away and we can see the star shining. Maybe it has a family of planets like the Sun.

145 **Stars begin their lives when they start making energy.** When the dust and gas pulls tightly together it gets very hot. Finally it gets so hot in the middle that it can start making energy. The energy makes the star shine, giving out heat and light like the Sun.

146
Young stars often stay together in clusters. When they start to shine they light up the nebula, making it glow with bright colours. Then the starlight blows away the remains of the cloud and we can see a group of new stars, called a star cluster.

▲ This cluster of young stars, with many stars of different colours and sizes, will gradually drift apart, breaking up the cluster.

QUIZ
1. What is a nebula?
2. How long has the Sun been shining?
3. What colour are large hot stars?
4. What is a group of new young stars called?

Answers:
1. a cloud of dust and gas in space 2. about 4 billion years 3. bluish-white 4. star cluster

148
Smaller stars live much longer than huge stars. Stars use up their gas to make energy, and the largest stars use up their gas much faster than smaller stars. The Sun is about half way through its life. It has been shining for about 5 billion years and will go on shining for another 5 billion years.

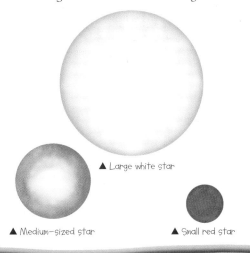

▲ Large white star

▲ Medium-sized star

▲ Small red star

147
Large stars are very hot and white, smaller stars are cooler and redder. A large star can make energy faster and get much hotter than a smaller star. This gives them a very bright, bluish-white colour. Smaller stars are cooler. This makes them look red and shine less brightly. Ordinary in-between stars like our Sun look yellow.

Death of a star

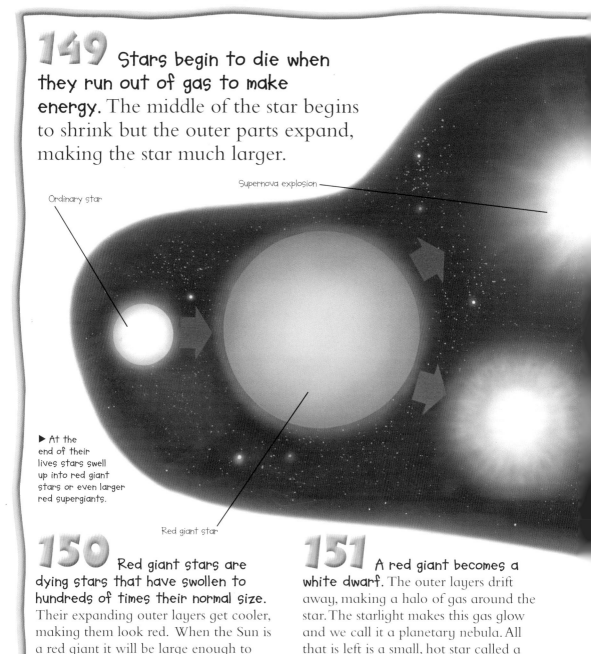

149 **Stars begin to die when they run out of gas to make energy.** The middle of the star begins to shrink but the outer parts expand, making the star much larger.

Ordinary star

Supernova explosion

▶ At the end of their lives stars swell up into red giant stars or even larger red supergiants.

Red giant star

150 **Red giant stars are dying stars that have swollen to hundreds of times their normal size.** Their expanding outer layers get cooler, making them look red. When the Sun is a red giant it will be large enough to swallow up the nearest planets, Mercury and Venus, and perhaps Earth.

151 **A red giant becomes a white dwarf.** The outer layers drift away, making a halo of gas around the star. The starlight makes this gas glow and we call it a planetary nebula. All that is left is a small, hot star called a white dwarf which cannot make energy and gradually cools and dies.

Black hole

152
Very heavy stars end their lives in a huge explosion called a supernova. This explosion blows away all the outer parts of the star. Gas rushes outwards in all directions, making a glowing shell. All that is left is a tiny hot star in the middle of the shell.

◀ After a supernova explosion, a giant star may end up as a very tiny hot star or even a black hole.

Black dwarf star

I DON'T BELIEVE IT!
Astronomers only know that black holes exist because they can see flickers of very hot gas near one just before they are sucked in.

153
After a supernova explosion the largest stars may end up as black holes. The remains of the star fall in on itself. As it shrinks, its gravity gets stronger. Eventually the pull of its gravity can get so strong that nothing near it can escape. This is called a black hole.

▲ When the Sun dies it will become 100 times bigger, then shrink down to 100 times smaller than it is now.

White dwarf star

Billions of galaxies

154 The Sun is part of a huge family of stars called the Milky Way Galaxy. There are billions of other stars in our Galaxy, as many as the grains of sand on a beach. We call it the Milky Way because it looks like a very faint band of light in the night sky, as though someone has spilt some milk across space.

▶ Seen from outside, our Galaxy would look like this. The Sun is towards the edge, in one of the spiral arms.

155 Curling arms give some galaxies their spiral shape. The Milky Way has arms made of bright stars and glowing clouds of gas which curl round into a spiral shape. Some galaxies, called elliptical galaxies, have a round shape like a squashed ball. Other galaxies have no particular shape.

I DON'T BELIEVE IT!
If you could fit the Milky Way onto these two pages, the Sun would be so tiny, you could not see it.

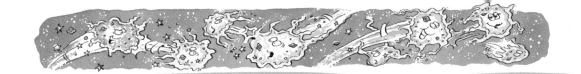

156 There are billions of galaxies outside the Milky Way. Some are larger than the Milky Way and many are smaller, but they all have more stars than you can count. The galaxies tend to stay together in groups called clusters.

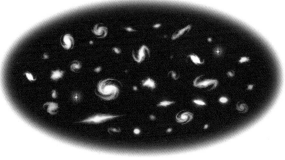

▲ A cluster of galaxies has many different types, with large elliptical and spiral galaxies and many small irregular ones.

▶ These two galaxies are so close that each has pulled a long tail of bright stars from the other.

157 There is no bump when galaxies collide. A galaxy is mostly empty space between the stars. But when galaxies get very close they can pull each other out of shape. Sometimes they look as if they have grown a huge tail stretching out into space, or their shape may change into a ring of glowing stars.

▼ From left to right these are spiral, irregular, and elliptical galaxies, and a spiral galaxy with a bar across the middle.

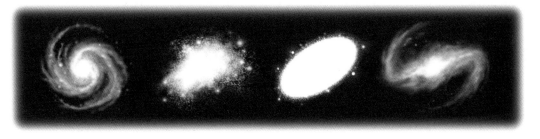

What is the Universe?

158 **The Universe is the name we give to everything we know about.** This means everything on Earth, from tiny bits of dust to the highest mountain, and everything that lives here, including you. It also means everything in space, all the billions of stars in the billions of galaxies.

159 **The Universe started with a massive explosion called the Big Bang.** Astronomers think that this happened about 15 billion years ago. A huge explosion sent everything racing outwards in all directions. To start with, everything was packed incredibly close together. Over time it has expanded (spread out) into the Universe we can see today, which is mostly empty space.

▼ 1. All the parts that make up the Universe were once packed tightly together. No one knows why the Universe started expanding with a Big Bang.

▼ 2. As everything moved apart in all directions, stars and galaxies started to form.

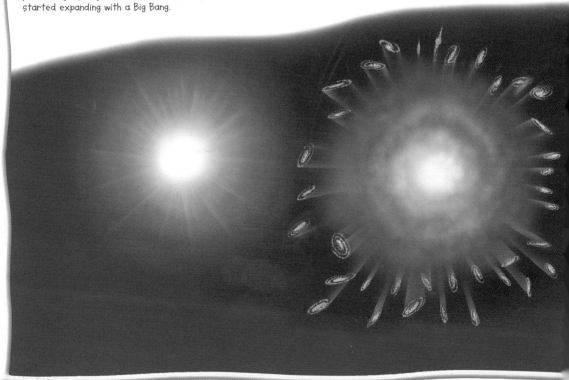

160
The galaxies are still racing away from each other. When astronomers look at distant galaxies, they can see other galaxies are moving away from our galaxy, and the more distant galaxies are moving away faster. In fact all the galaxies are moving apart from each other. We say that the Universe is expanding.

161
We do not know what will happen to the Universe billions of years from now. It may keep on expanding. If this happens, old stars will gradually die and no new ones will be born. Everywhere will be dark and cold.

▼ 3. Today there are galaxies of different shapes and sizes, all moving apart. One day they may start moving towards each other.

162
The Universe may end with a Big Crunch. This means that the galaxies would all start coming closer together. In the end the galaxies and stars would all be crushed together in a Big Crunch, the opposite of the Big Bang explosion.

DOTTY UNIVERSE
You will need:
a balloon
Blow up a balloon a little, holding the neck to stop air escaping. Mark dots on the balloon with a pen, then blow it up some more. Watch how the dots move apart from each other. This is like the galaxies moving apart as the Universe expands.

▼ 4. The Universe could end as it began, all packed incredibly close together.

Looking into space

163 People have imagined they can see the outlines of people and animals in star patterns in the sky. These patterns are constellations. Astromomers named the constellations to help them find their way around the skies.

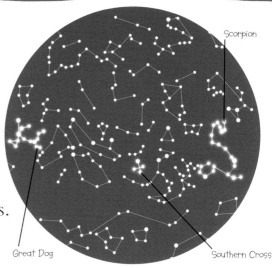

Scorpion

Great Dog

Southern Cross

▲ If you live south of the Equator, these are the constellations you can see at night.

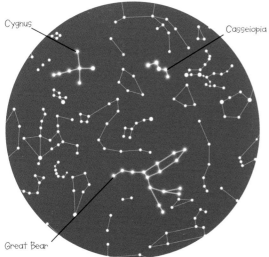

Cygnus

Casseiopia

Great Bear

▲ From the north of the Equator, you can see a different set of constellations in the night sky.

Dome

Control room

Telescope

164 Astronomers use huge telescopes to see much more than we can see with just our eyes. Telescopes make things look bigger and nearer. They also show faint, glowing clouds of gas, and distant stars and galaxies.

▲ A huge dome protects this large telescope. It opens to let the telescope point at the sky, and both the dome and telescope can turn to look at any part of the sky.

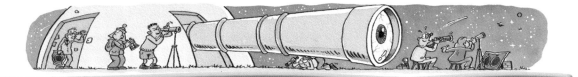

▲ The Hubble Space Telescope takes much more detailed pictures and can see farther than any similar telescope.

165 Space telescopes look even further to find exciting things in deep space. On Earth, clouds often hide the stars and the air is always moving, which blurs the pictures made by the telescopes. A telescope in space above the air can make clearer pictures. The Hubble Space Telescope has been circling the Earth for more than 10 years sending back beautiful pictures.

166 Astronomers also look at radio signals from space. They use telescopes that look like huge satellite TV dishes. These make pictures using the radio signals that come from space. The pictures do not always look like those from ordinary telescopes, but they can spot exciting things that most ordinary telescopes cannot see, such as jets of gas from black holes.

MOON-WATCH
You will need:
binoculars
On a clear night look at the Moon through binoculars, holding them very steady. You will be able to see the round shapes of craters. Binoculars are really two telescopes, one for each eye, and they make the Moon look bigger so you can see more detail.

▼ Radio telescopes often have rows of dishes like these to collect radio signals from space. Altogether, they act like one much larger dish to make more detailed pictures. The dishes can move to look in any direction.

Three, two, one... Lift-off!

167 To blast into space, a rocket has to travel nearly 40 times faster than a jumbo jet. If it goes any slower, gravity pulls it back to Earth. Rockets are powered by burning fuel, which makes hot gases. These gases rush out of the engines, shooting the rocket forwards.

▶ The huge *Ariane 5* rocket can launch two satellites at once.

Satellite goes into space

▶ Each stage fires its engine to make the rocket go faster and faster until it puts the satellite into space.

Third stage

First stage

Second stage

Booster rockets drop away

168 A single rocket is not powerful enough to launch a satellite or spacecraft into space. So rockets have two or three stages, which are really separate rockets mounted on top of each other, each with its own engines. When the first stage has used up its fuel it drops away, and the second stage starts. Finally the third stage takes over to go into space.

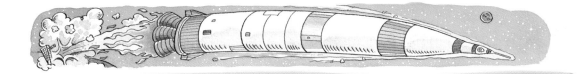

169

The space shuttle takes off from Earth as a rocket. It has rocket engines that burn fuel from a huge tank. But it also needs two large booster rockets to give it extra speed. The boosters drop away after two minutes, and the main rocket tank after six.

ROCKET POWER

You will need:

a balloon

If you blow up a balloon and let it go, the balloon shoots off across the room. The air inside the balloon has rushed out, pushing the balloon away in the opposite direction. A rocket blasting into space works in a similar way.

170

The shuttle lands back on Earth on a long runway, just like a giant glider. It does not use any engines for the landing, unlike an aircraft. It touches down so fast, the pilot uses a parachute as well as brakes to stop it on the runway.

◄ The shuttle puts down its wheels and lands on the runway.

▲ The shuttle is blasted into space by three rocket engines and two huge booster rockets.

Living in space

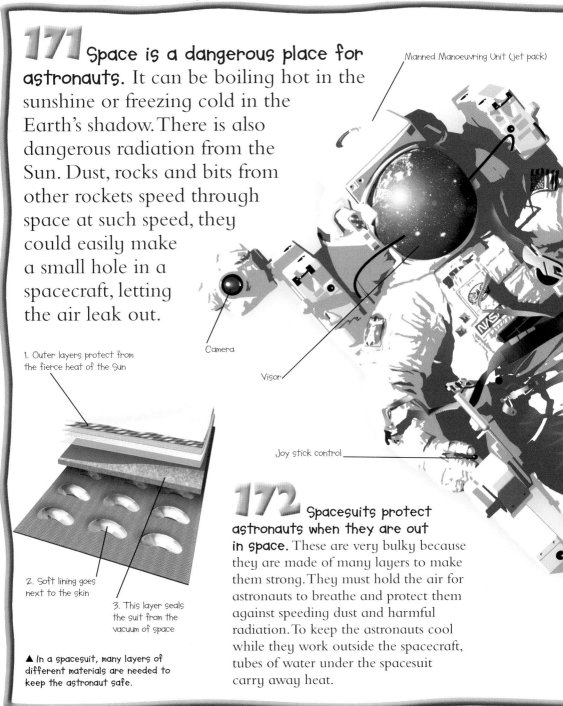

171 **Space is a dangerous place for astronauts.** It can be boiling hot in the sunshine or freezing cold in the Earth's shadow. There is also dangerous radiation from the Sun. Dust, rocks and bits from other rockets speed through space at such speed, they could easily make a small hole in a spacecraft, letting the air leak out.

Manned Manoeuvring Unit (jet pack)

Camera

Visor

Joy stick control

1. Outer layers protect from the fierce heat of the Sun

2. Soft lining goes next to the skin

3. This layer seals the suit from the vacuum of space

▲ In a spacesuit, many layers of different materials are needed to keep the astronaut safe.

172 **Spacesuits protect astronauts when they are out in space.** These are very bulky because they are made of many layers to make them strong. They must hold the air for astronauts to breathe and protect them against speeding dust and harmful radiation. To keep the astronauts cool while they work outside the spacecraft, tubes of water under the spacesuit carry away heat.

SPACE MEALS

You will need:

dried noodles

Buy a dried snack such as noodles, that just needs boiling water added. This is the kind of food astronauts eat. Most of their meals are dried so they are not too heavy to launch into space.

173
Everything floats around in space as if it had no weight. So all objects have to be fixed down or they will float away. Astronauts have footholds to keep them still while they are working. They strap themselves into sleeping bags so they don't bump into things when they are asleep.

Glove

Spacesuit

▲ Sleeping bags are fixed to a wall so astronauts look as though they are asleep standing up.

174
Astronauts must take everything they need into space with them. Out in space there is no air, water or food so all the things that astronauts need to live must be packed into their spacecraft and taken with them.

Home from home

175 A space station is a home in space for astronauts and cosmonauts (Russian astronauts). It has a kitchen for making meals, and cabins with sleeping bags. There are toilets, wash basins and sometimes showers. They have places to work and controls where astronauts can check that everything is working properly.

Solar panels for power

176 The International Space Station, ISS, is being built in space. This is the latest and largest space station. Sixteen countries are helping to build it including the US, Russia, Japan, Canada, Brazil and 11 European countries. It is built up from separate sections called modules that have been made to fit together like a jigsaw.

Docking port

I DON'T BELIEVE IT!
The US space station *Skylab*, launched in 1973, fell back to Earth in 1979. Most of it landed in the ocean but some pieces hit Australia.

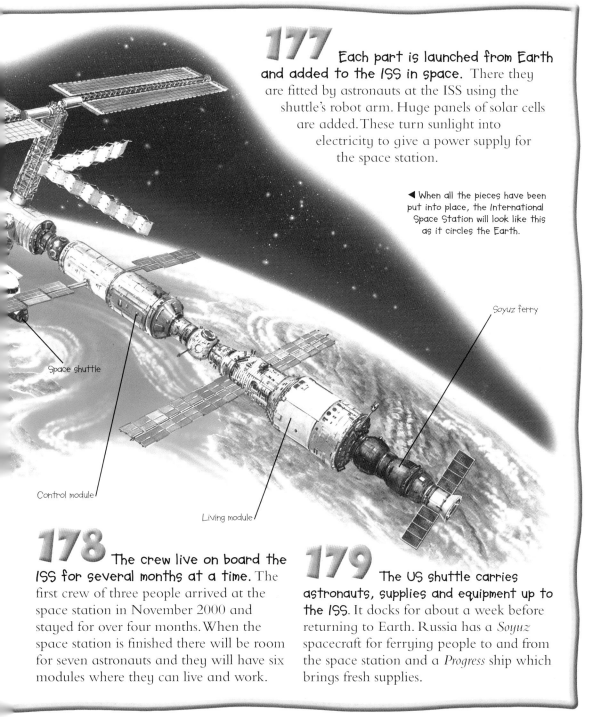

177 Each part is launched from Earth and added to the ISS in space. There they are fitted by astronauts at the ISS using the shuttle's robot arm. Huge panels of solar cells are added. These turn sunlight into electricity to give a power supply for the space station.

◄ When all the pieces have been put into place, the International Space Station will look like this as it circles the Earth.

Soyuz ferry

Space shuttle

Control module

Living module

178 The crew live on board the ISS for several months at a time. The first crew of three people arrived at the space station in November 2000 and stayed for over four months. When the space station is finished there will be room for seven astronauts and they will have six modules where they can live and work.

179 The US shuttle carries astronauts, supplies and equipment up to the ISS. It docks for about a week before returning to Earth. Russia has a *Soyuz* spacecraft for ferrying people to and from the space station and a *Progress* ship which brings fresh supplies.

Robot explorers

180 **Robot spacecraft called probes have explored all the planets except Pluto.** Probes travel in space to take close-up pictures and measurements. They send the information back to scientists on Earth. Some probes circle planets taking pictures. For a really close-up look, a probe can land on the surface.

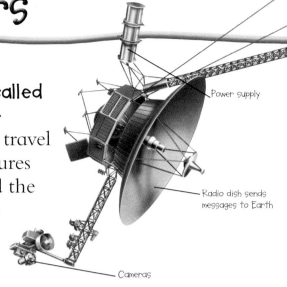

Power supply

Radio dish sends messages to Earth

Cameras

▲ *Voyager 2* gave us close-up pictures of four different planets.

181 **In 1976, two *Viking* spacecraft landed on Mars to look for life.** They scooped up some dust and tested it to see if any tiny creatures lived on Mars. They did not find any signs of life and their pictures showed only a dry, red, dusty desert.

▼ The *Viking* landers took soil samples from Mars, but found no sign of life.

182 **Two *Voyager* probes left Earth in 1977 to visit the gas giant planets.** They reached Jupiter in 1979, flying past and on to Saturn. *Voyager 2* went on to visit Uranus and then Neptune in 1989. It sent back thousands of pictures of each planet as it flew past.

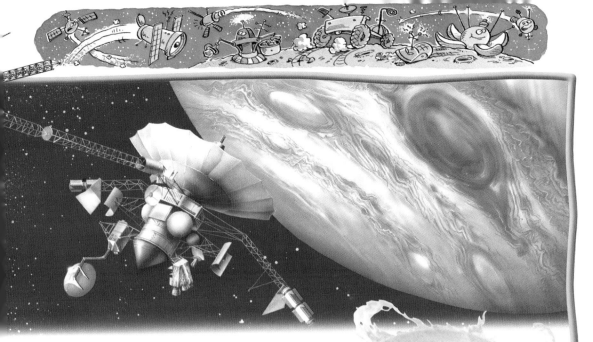

▲ When *Galileo* has finished sending back pictures of Jupiter and its moons, it will plunge into Jupiter's swirling clouds.

183
Galileo has circled Jupiter for more than six years.
It arrived in 1995 and dropped a small probe into Jupiter's clouds. Galileo sent back pictures of the planet and its largest moons. It was discovered that two of them may have water hidden under ice thicker than the Arctic ice on Earth.

◀ *Sojourner* spent three months on Mars. The small rover was about the size of a microwave oven.

QUIZ
1. When did the *Voyager* probes fly past Jupiter?
2. Which probe sent pictures of Jupiter's clouds?
3. Which probes tested the dust on Mars for signs of life?
4. What was the name of the *Mars Pathfinder* rover?

Answers:
1. 1979 2. *Galileo*
3. *Viking* 4. *Sojourner*

184
Mars Pathfinder carried a small rover called *Sojourner* to Mars in 1997. It landed on the surface and opened up to let *Sojourner* out. This rover was like a remote control car, but with six wheels. It tested the soil and rocks to find out what they were made of as it slowly drove around the landing site.

Watching the Earth

185 **Hundreds of satellites circle the Earth in space.** They are launched into space by rockets and may stay there for ten years or more.

▶ Weather satellites look down at the clouds and give warning when a violent storm is approaching.

186 **Communications satellites carry TV programmes and telephone messages around the world.** Large aerials on Earth beam radio signals up to a space satellite which then beams them down to another aerial, half way round the world. This lets us talk to people on the other side of the world, and watch events such as the Olympics Games while they are happening in faraway countries.

▼ Communications satellites can beam TV programmes directly to your home through your own aerial dish.

187 **Weather satellites help the forecasters tell us what the weather will be like.** These satellites can see where the clouds are forming and which way they are going. They watch the winds and rain and measure how hot the air and the ground are.

▶ The different satellites each have their own job to do, looking at the Earth, or the weather, or out into space.

188
Earth-watching satellites look out for pollution. Oil slicks in the sea and dirty air over cities show up clearly in pictures from these satellites. They can help farmers by watching how well crops are growing and by looking for pests and diseases. Spotting forest fires and icebergs that may be a danger to ships is also easier from space.

▼ Pictures of the Earth taken by satellites can help make very accurate maps.

▲ Satellite telescopes let astronomers look far out into the Universe and discover what is out there.

189
Satellite telescopes let astronomers look at exciting things in space. They can see other kinds of radiation, such as x-rays, as well as light. X-ray telescopes can tell astronomers where there may be a black hole.

I DON'T BELIEVE IT!
Spy satellites circling the Earth take pictures of secret sites around the world. They can listen to secret radio messages from military ships or aircraft.

Voyage to the Moon

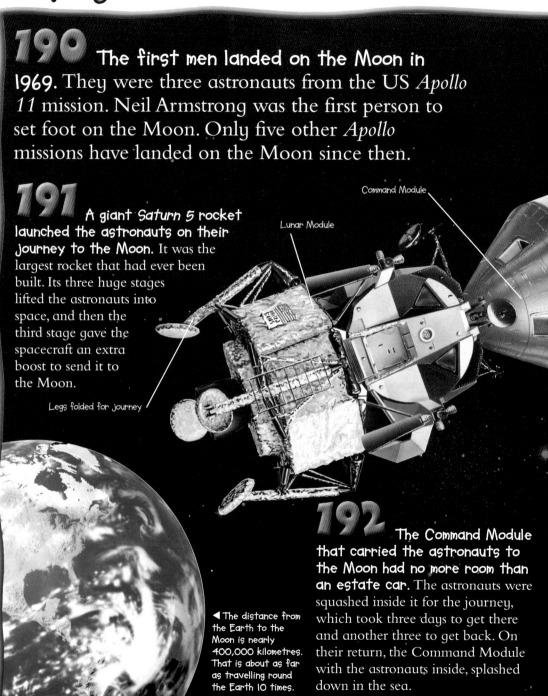

190 **The first men landed on the Moon in 1969.** They were three astronauts from the US *Apollo 11* mission. Neil Armstrong was the first person to set foot on the Moon. Only five other *Apollo* missions have landed on the Moon since then.

191 **A giant *Saturn 5* rocket launched the astronauts on their journey to the Moon.** It was the largest rocket that had ever been built. Its three huge stages lifted the astronauts into space, and then the third stage gave the spacecraft an extra boost to send it to the Moon.

Command Module

Lunar Module

Legs folded for journey

192 **The Command Module that carried the astronauts to the Moon had no more room than an estate car.** The astronauts were squashed inside it for the journey, which took three days to get there and another three to get back. On their return, the Command Module with the astronauts inside, splashed down in the sea.

◄ The distance from the Earth to the Moon is nearly 400,000 kilometres. That is about as far as travelling round the Earth 10 times.

▶ The longest time that any of the *Apollo* missions stayed on the Moon was just over three days.

Thrusters

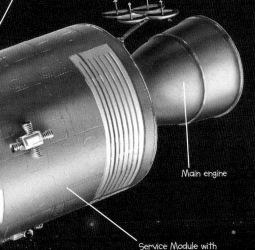

Main engine

Service Module with fuel and air supplies

▲ The Lunar and Command Modules travelled to the Moon fixed together, then separated for the Moon landing.

194 The Lunar Rover was a moon car for the astronauts to ride on. It looked like a buggy with four wheels and two seats. It could only travel about as fast as you can run.

195 No one has been back to the Moon since the last *Apollo* mission left in 1972. Astronauts had visited six different places on the Moon and brought back enough Moon rock to keep scientists busy for many years. Maybe one day people will return to the Moon and build bases where they can live and work.

193 The Lunar Module took two of the astronauts to the Moon's surface. Once safely landed they put on spacesuits and went outside to collect rocks. Later they took off in the Lunar Module to join the third astronaut who had stayed in the Command Module, circling above the Moon on his own.

I DON'T BELIEVE IT!
On the way to the Moon an explosion damaged the *Apollo* 13 spacecraft, leaving the astronauts with little heat or light.

Are we alone?

196 **The only life we have found so far in the Universe is here on Earth.** Everywhere you look on Earth from the frozen Antarctic to the hottest, driest deserts, on land and in the sea, there are living things. Some are huge, such as whales and elephants and others are much too small to see. But they all need water to live.

▲ On Earth, animals can live in many different habitats, such as in the sea, the air, in deserts and jungles, and icy lands. How many different habitats can you see here?

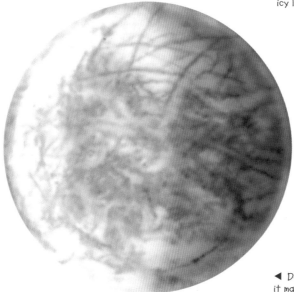

197 **There may be an underground ocean on Europa, one of Jupiter's moons.** Europa is a little smaller than our Moon and is covered in ice. However, astronomers think that there may be an ocean of water under the ice. If so, there could be strange living creatures swimming around deep underground.

◄ Deep beneath the cracked, icy surface of Europa, it may be warm enough for the ice to melt into water.

198
Astronomers have found signs of planets circling other stars, but none like the Earth so far. The planets they have found are large ones like Jupiter, but they keep looking for a planet with a solid surface which is not too hot or too cold. They are looking for one where there might be water and living things.

▲ No one knows what other planets would be like. They could have strange moons or colourful rings. Anything that lives there might look very strange to us.

199
Mars seems to have had rivers and seas billions of years ago. Astronomers can see dry river beds and ridges that look like ocean shores on Mars. This makes them think Mars may have been warm and wet long ago and something may have lived there. Now it is very cold and dry with no sign of life.

◄ This message could tell people living on distant planets about the Earth, and the people who live here.

I DON'T BELIEVE IT!
It would take thousands of years to get to the nearest stars with our present spacecraft.

200
Scientists have sent a radio message to a distant group of stars. They are hoping that anyone living there will understand the message about life on Earth. However, it will take 25,000 years to get to the stars and another 25,000 years for a reply to come back to Earth!

Water world

201 Oceans cover over two-thirds of the Earth's rocky surface. Their total area is about 362 million square kilometres, which means there is more than twice as much ocean as land! Although all the oceans flow into each other, we know them as four different oceans – the Pacific, Atlantic, Indian and Arctic. Our landmasses, the continents, rise out of the oceans.

Arctic Ocean

Atlantic Ocean

Pacific Ocean

Atlantic Ocean

202 The largest, deepest ocean is the Pacific. It covers nearly half of our planet and is almost as big as the other three oceans put together! In places, the Pacific is so deep that the Earth's tallest mountain, Everest, would sink without a trace.

The deepest parts of the Pacific would cover Mount Everest without trace

▶ Mount Everest is the highest point on Earth, rising to 8848 metres. Parts of the Pacific Ocean are deeper than 10,000 metres.

Light hits the surface of the water

► A cup of sea water appears see-through. It is only when you look at a large area of sea that it has colour.

Scattered blue and green

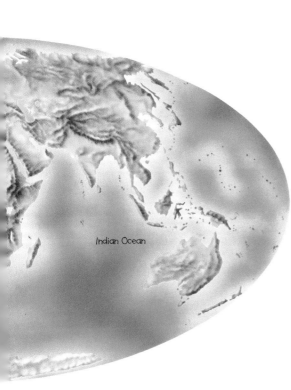

Indian Ocean

▲ The world's oceans cover most of our planet. Each ocean is made up of smaller bodies of water called seas.

203 Oceans can look blue, green or grey. This is because of the way light hits the surface. Water soaks up the red parts of light but scatters the blue-green parts, making the sea look different shades of blue or green.

204 Seas can be red or dead. A sea is a small part of an ocean. The Red Sea, for example, is the part of the Indian Ocean between Egypt and Saudi Arabia. Asia's Dead Sea isn't a true sea, but a landlocked lake. We call it a sea because it is a large body of water.

205 There are streams in the oceans. All the water in the oceans is constantly moving, but in some places it flows as currents, which take particular paths. One of these is the warm Gulf Stream, that travels around the edge of the Atlantic Ocean.

I DON'T BELIEVE IT!
97 percent of the world's water is in the oceans. Just a fraction is in freshwater lakes and rivers.

Ocean features

206 There are plains, mountains and valleys under the oceans, in areas called basins. Each basin has a rim (the flat continental shelf that meets the shore) and sides (the continental slope that drops away from the shelf). In the ocean basin there are flat abyssal plains, steep hills, huge underwater volcanoes called seamounts, and deep valleys called trenches.

▼ Magma (molten rock) escapes from the seabed to form a ridge. This ridge has collapsed to form a rift valley.

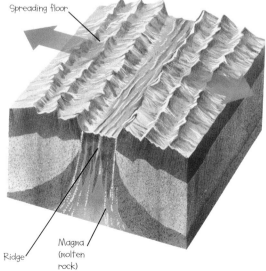

Spreading floor

Ridge

Magma (molten rock)

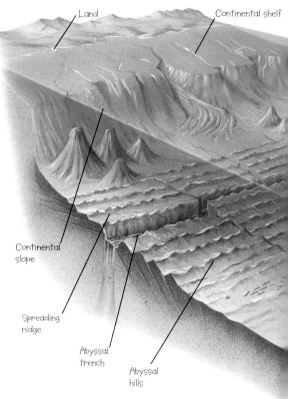

Land

Continental shelf

Continental slope

Spreading ridge

Abyssal trench

Abyssal hills

▲ Under the oceans there is a landscape similar to that found on land.

207 The ocean floor is spreading. Molten (liquid) rock inside the Earth seeps from holes on the seabed. As the rock cools, it forms new sections of floor that creep slowly out. Scientists have proved this fact by looking at layers of rock on the ocean floor. There are matching stripes of rock either side of a ridge. Each pair came from the same hot rock eruption, then slowly spread out.

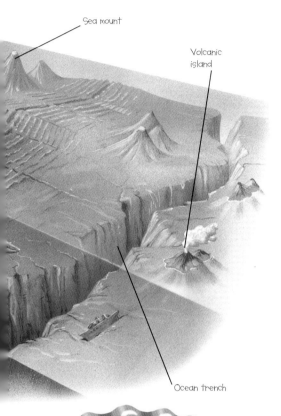

Sea mount

Volcanic island

Ocean trench

▼ An atoll is a ring–shaped coral reef that encloses a deep lagoon. It can form when a volcanic island sinks underwater.

1. Coral starts to grow

4. Coral atoll is left behind

2. Lagoon appears around volcano

3. Volcano disappears

208 Some islands are swallowed by the ocean. Sometimes, a ring-shaped coral reef called an atoll marks where an island once was. The coral reef built up around the island. After the volcano blew its top, the reef remained.

▶ There are more Hawaiian islands still to come – Loihi is just visible beneath the water's surface.

209 New islands are born all the time. When an underwater volcano erupts, its lava cools in the water. Layers of lava build up, and the volcano gets bigger. Eventually, it is tall enough to peep above the waves. The Hawaiian islands rose from the sea like this.

Tides and shores

210 **The sea level rises and falls twice each day along the coast.** This is known as high and low tides. Tides happen because of the pull of the Moon, which lifts water from the part of the Earth's surface facing it.

▼ At high tide, the sea rises up the shore and dumps seaweed, shells and drift wood. Most coasts have two high tides and two low tides every day.

High tides happen at the same time each day on opposite sides of the Earth

At high tide the water level rises

At low tide the water level goes down again

211 **Spring tides are especially high.** They occur twice a month, when the Moon is in line with the Earth and the Sun. Then, the Sun's pulling force joins the Moon's and seawater is lifted higher than usual. The opposite happens when the Moon and Sun are at right angles to the Earth. Then, their pulling powers work against each other causing weak neap tides – the lowest high tides and low tides.

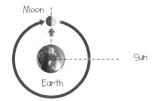

Moon

Sun

Earth

◄ Neap tides occur when the Sun and Moon are at right angles to each other and pulling in different directions.

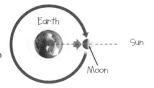

Earth

Sun

Moon

► Spring tides occur when the Sun and the Moon are lined up and pulling together.

212 The sea is strong enough to carve into rock. Pounding waves batter coastlines and erode, or wear away, the rock.

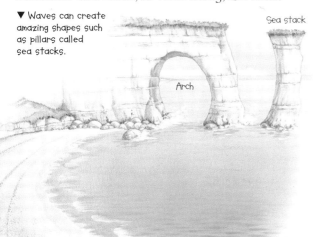

▼ Waves can create amazing shapes such as pillars called sea stacks.

Sea stack

Arch

▲ A tsunami can travel faster than a jumbo jet.

215 Tidal waves are the most powerful waves. Also known as tsunamis, they happen when underwater earthquakes trigger tremendous shock waves. These whip up a wall of water that travels across the sea's surface.

213 Sand is found on bars and spits, as well as beaches. It is made up of grains of worn-down rock and shell. Sand collects on shorelines and spits, but also forms on offshore beaches called sand bars. Spits are narrow ridges of worn sand and pebbles.

I DON'T BELIEVE IT!
The biggest tsunami was taller than five Statues of Liberty! It hit the Japanese Ryuku Islands in 1771.

214 Some shores are swampy. This makes the border between land and sea hard to pinpoint. Muddy coastlines include tropical mangrove swamps that are flooded by salty water from the sea.

▶ The stilt-like roots of mangrove trees take in both air and water.

Life in a rock pool

216 Rock pools are teeming with all kinds of creatures. Limpets are a kind of shellfish. They live on rocks and in pools at shorelines. Here, they eat slimy, green algae, but they have to withstand the crashing tide. They cling to the rock with their muscular foot, only moving when the tide is out.

217 Some anemones fight with harpoons. Beadlet anemones will sometimes fight over a feeding ground. Their weapon is the poison they usually use to stun their prey. They shoot tiny hooks like harpoons at each other until the weakest one gives in.

▲ Anemones are named after flowers, because of their petal-like arms.

218 Starfish can grow new arms. They may have as many as 40 arms, or rays. If a predator grabs hold of one, the starfish abandons the ray, and uses the others to make its getaway!

◀ Starfish are relatives of brittle stars, sea urchins and sea cucumbers.

219
Hermit crabs do not have shells. Most crabs shed their shells as they outgrow them, but the hermit crab does not have a shell. It borrows the leftover shell of a dead whelk or other mollusc – whatever it can squeeze into to protect its soft body. These crabs have even been spotted using a coconut shell as a home!

▶ Hermit crabs protect their soft bodies in a borrowed shell.

FIND THE SHELL
Can you find the names of four shells in the puzzle below ?

1. **alcm** 2. **lesmus**
3. **teroys** 4. **hewkl**

Answers:
1. Clam 2. Mussel
3. Oyster 4. Whelk

220
Sea urchins wear a disguise. Green sea urchins sometimes drape themselves with bits of shell, pebble and seaweed. This makes the urchin more difficult for predators, or hunters, to spot.

◀ There are about 4500 different types of sponge in the sea.

221
Sponges are animals! They are very simple creatures that filter their food from sea water. The natural sponge that you might use in the bath is a long-dead, dried-out sponge.

Colourful coral

222 **Tiny animals build huge underwater walls.** These are built up from coral, the leftover skeletons of sea creatures called polyps. Over millions of years, enough skeletons pile up to form huge, wall-like structures called reefs. Coral reefs are full of hidey-holes and make brilliant habitats for all sorts of amazing, colourful sea life.

223 **The world's biggest shellfish lives on coral reefs.** Giant clams grow to well over one metre long – big enough for you to bathe in its shell!

224 **Seahorse dads have the babies.** They don't exactly give birth, but they store the eggs in a pouch on their belly. When the eggs are ready to hatch, a stream of miniature seahorses billows out from the dad's pouch.

▶ Baby seahorses stream out of their father's pouch and into the sea.

Parrot fish

Giant clam

Clownfish

225
Some fish go to the cleaners.
Cleaner wrasse are little fish that are paid for cleaning! Larger fish, such as groupers and moray eels visit the wrasse, which nibble all the parasites and other bits of dirt off the bigger fishes' bodies – what a feast!

226
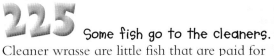 **Clownfish are sting–proof.**
Most creatures steer clear of an anemone's stinging tentacles. But the clownfish swims among the stingers, where it's safe from predators. Strangely, the anemone doesn't seem to sting the clownfish.

Lion fish

Cleaner wrasse fish

I DON'T BELIEVE IT!
You can see the Great Barrier Reef from space! At over 2000 km long, it is the largest structure ever built by living creatures.

227
 **Some fish look like stones.** Stone fish rest on the seabed, looking just like the rocks that surround them. If they are spotted, the poisonous spines on their backs can stun an attacker in seconds.

Stone fish

▲ Tropical coral reefs are the habitat of an amazing range of marine plants and creatures.

Swimming machines

228 There are over 21,000 different types of fish in the sea. They range from huge whale sharks to tiny gobies. Almost all are covered in scales and use fins and a muscular tail to power through the water. Like their freshwater cousins, sea fish have slits called gills that take oxygen from the water so they can breathe.

229 The oarfish is bigger than an oar – it is as long as four canoes! It is the longest bony fish and is found in all the world's oceans. Oarfish are handsome creatures – they have a striking red fin along the length of their back.

◀ People once thought oarfish swam horizontally through the water. Now they know they swim upright.

▶ At over three metres long, sunfish are the biggest bony fish in the oceans. They feed on plankton.

230 Sunfish like sunbathing! Ocean sunfish are very large, broad fish that can weigh as much as a tonne. They are named after their habit of sunbathing on the surface of the open ocean.

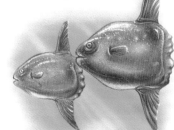

▶ Flying fish feed near the surface so they are easy to find. Their gliding flight helps them escape most hunters.

232 Flying fish cannot really fly.

Fish can't survive out of water, but flying fish sometimes leap above the waves when they are travelling at high speeds. They use their wing-like fins to keep them in the air for as long as 30 seconds.

▲ In a large group called a school, fish like these yellow snappers have less chance of being picked off by a predator.

231 Not all fish are the

same shape. Cod or mackerel are what we think of as a normal fish shape, but fish come in all shapes and sizes. Flounder and other flatfish have squashed-flat bodies. Eels are so long and thin that the biggest types look like snakes, while tiny garden eels resemble worms! And of course, seahorses and seadragons look nothing like other fish at all!

▶ The flounder's flattened shape and dull colouring help to camouflage (hide) it on the seabed.

QUIZ
1. Which fish like to sunbathe?
2. How many types of fish live in the sea?
3. How does a fish breathe?
4. Can flying fish really fly?

Answers:
1. Sunfish 2. 21,000 3. With its gills 4. No

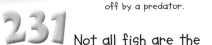

Shark!

233 Great whites are the scariest sharks in the oceans. These powerful predators have been known to kill people and can speed through the water at 30 kilometres per hour. Unlike most fish, the great white is warm-blooded. This allows its muscles to work well, but also means the shark has to feed on plenty of meat.

▼ Basking sharks eat enormous amounts of plankton. They sieve through around 1000 tonnes of water every hour.

▲ Great white sharks are fierce hunters. They will attack and eat almost anything, but prefer to feed on seals.

234 Most sharks are meat-eaters. Herring are a favourite food for sand tiger and thresher sharks, while a hungry tiger shark will gobble up just about anything! Strangely, some of the biggest sharks take the smallest prey. Whale sharks and basking sharks eat tiny sea creatures called plankton.

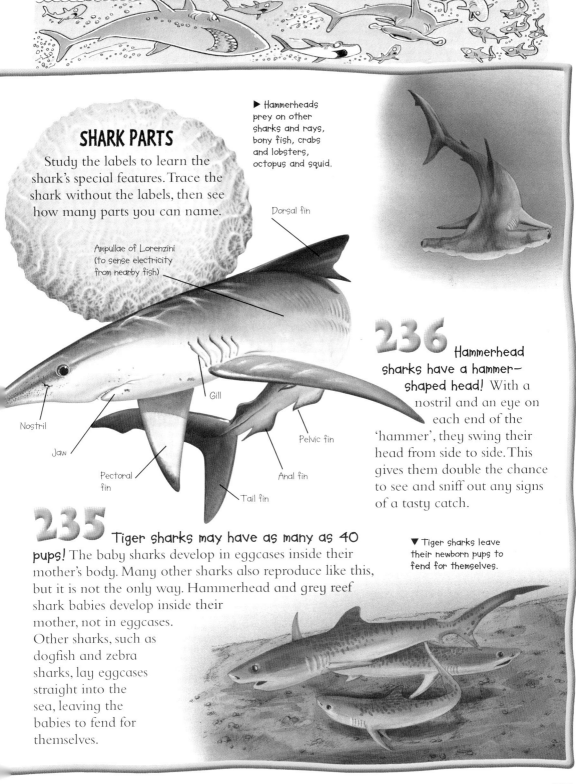

SHARK PARTS

Study the labels to learn the shark's special features. Trace the shark without the labels, then see how many parts you can name.

► Hammerheads prey on other sharks and rays, bony fish, crabs and lobsters, octopus and squid.

Dorsal fin

Ampullae of Lorenzini (to sense electricity from nearby fish)

Gill

Nostril

Jaw

Pectoral fin

Pelvic fin

Anal fin

Tail fin

236 Hammerhead sharks have a hammer-shaped head! With a nostril and an eye on each end of the 'hammer', they swing their head from side to side. This gives them double the chance to see and sniff out any signs of a tasty catch.

235 Tiger sharks may have as many as 40 pups! The baby sharks develop in eggcases inside their mother's body. Many other sharks also reproduce like this, but it is not the only way. Hammerhead and grey reef shark babies develop inside their mother, not in eggcases. Other sharks, such as dogfish and zebra sharks, lay eggcases straight into the sea, leaving the babies to fend for themselves.

▼ Tiger sharks leave their newborn pups to fend for themselves.

Whales and dolphins

237 **The biggest animal on the planet lives in the oceans.** It is the blue whale, measuring about 28 metres in length and weighing up to 190 tonnes. It feeds by filtering tiny, shrimp-like creatures called krill from the water – about four tonnes of krill a day! Like other great whales, it has special, sieve-like parts in its mouth called baleen plates.

▲ As the sperm whale surfaces, it pushes out stale air through its blowhole. It fills its lungs with fresh air and dives down again.

238 **Whales and dolphins have to come to the surface for air.** This is because they are mammals, like we are. Sperm whales hold their breath the longest. They have been known to stay underwater for nearly two hours.

▲ Blue whale calves feed on their mother's rich milk until they are around eight months old.

241 **Killer whales play with their food.** They especially like to catch baby seals, which they toss into the air before eating. Killer whales are not true whales, but the largest dolphins. They have teeth for chewing, instead of baleen plates.

▲ Killer whales carry the baby seals out to sea before eating them.

▶ The beluga is a type of white whale. It makes a range of noises – whistles, clangs, chirps and moos!

239 **Dolphins and whales sing songs to communicate.** The noisiest is the humpback whale, whose wailing noises can be heard for hundreds of kilometres. The sweetest is the beluga – nicknamed the 'sea canary'. Songs are used to attract a mate, or just to keep track of each other.

242 **Moby Dick was a famous white whale.** It starred in a book by Herman Melville about a white sperm whale and a whaler called Captain Ahab.

240 **The narwhal has a horn like a unicorn's.** This Arctic whale has a long, twirly tooth that spirals out of its head. The males use their tusks as a weapon when they are fighting over females.

I DON'T BELIEVE IT!
Barnacles are shellfish. They attach themselves to ships' hulls, or the bodies of grey whales and other large sea animals.

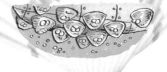

▲ The narwhal's three-metre tusk seems too long for its body.

Ocean reptiles

247 **Marine iguanas are the most seaworthy lizards.** Most lizards prefer life on land, where it is easier to warm up their cold-blooded bodies, but marine iguanas depend on the sea for their food. They dive underwater to graze on the algae and seaweed growing on rocks.

▲ Marine iguanas are found around the Galapagos Islands in the Pacific. When they are not diving for food, they bask on the rocks that dot the island coastlines. The lizards' dark skin helps to absorb the Sun's heat.

248 **Turtles come ashore only to lay their eggs.** Although they are born on land, turtles head for the sea the minute they hatch. Females return to the beach where they were born to dig their nest. After they have laid their eggs, they go straight back to the water. Hawksbill turtles may lay up to 140 eggs in a clutch, while some green turtle females clock up 800 eggs in a year!

▲ In a single breeding season, a female green turtle may lay as many as ten clutches, each containing up to 80 eggs!

249 There are venomous (poisonous) snakes in the sea. Most stay close to land and come ashore to lay their eggs. Banded sea snakes, for example, cruise around coral reefs in search of their favourite food, eels. But the yellow-bellied sea snake never leaves the water. It gives birth to live babies in the open ocean.

▼ Banded sea snakes use venom (poison) to stun prey, but the yellow-bellied sea snake has a sneakier trick. Once its colourful underside has attracted some fish, it darts back – so the fish are next to its open mouth! The venom of sea snakes is more powerful than that of any land snake.

Banded sea snake

Yellow-bellied sea snake

MIX AND MATCH
Can you match these sea turtles to their names?

1. Green 2. Hawksbill
3. Leatherback 4. Loggerhead

Answers:
1C 2B 3D 4A

a.

b.

c.

d.

▼ Leatherbacks are the biggest turtles in the world and can grow to four metres in length.

250 Leatherbacks dive up to 1200 metres for dinner. These turtles hold the record for being the biggest sea turtles and for making the deepest dives. Leatherbacks feed mostly on jellyfish but their diet also includes molluscs, crabs and lobsters, starfish and sea urchins.

Icy depths

251 **Few creatures can survive in the dark, icy-cold ocean depths.** Food is so hard to come by, the deep-sea anglerfish does not waste energy chasing prey — it has developed a clever fishing trick. A stringy 'fishing rod' with a glowing tip extends from its dorsal fin or hangs above its jaw. This attracts smaller fish to the anglerfish's big mouth.

▼ Anglerfish are black or brown for camouflage. Only their glowing 'fishing rod' is visible in the gloom.

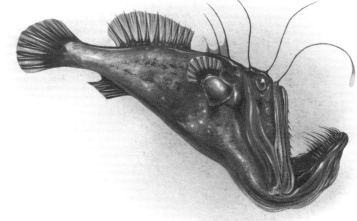

▼ The light created by deep-sea fish, or by bacteria living on their bodies, is known as biological light, or bioluminescence.

Lantern fish

Cookiecutter shark

Dragon fish

252 **Some deep-sea fish glow in the dark.** As well as tempting prey, light also confuses predators. About 1500 different deep-sea fish give off light. The lantern fish's whole body glows, while the dragon fish has light organs dotted along its sides and belly. Just the belly of the cookiecutter shark gives off a ghostly glow. Cookiecutters take biscuit-shaped bites out of their prey's body!

253
Black swallowers are real greedy-guts! These strange fish are just 25 centimetres long but can eat fish far bigger than themselves. Their loose jaws unhinge to fit over the prey. Then the stretchy body expands to take in their enormous meal.

▼ Like many deep-sea fish, black swallowers have smooth, scaleless skin.

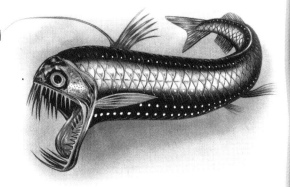

▲ The viperfish is named for its long, snake-like fangs.

254
Viperfish have teeth which are invisible in the dark. They swim around with their jaws wide open. Deep-sea shrimp often see nothing until they are right inside the viperfish's mouth.

▶ Tubeworms grow around deep-sea volcanoes called black smokers.

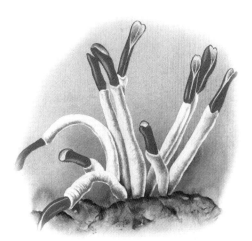

I DON'T BELIEVE IT!
Female deep-sea anglerfish grow to 120 centimetres in length, but the males are a tiny six centimetres!

255
On the seabed, there are worms as long as cars! These are giant tubeworms and they cluster around hot spots on the ocean floor. They feed on tiny particles that they filter from the water.

Amazing journeys

256 Many ocean animals travel incredible distances. Spiny lobsters spend the summer feeding off the coast of Florida, but head south in autumn to deeper waters. They travel about 50 kilometres along the seabed, in columns that may be more than 50-strong. They keep together by touch, using their long, spiky antennae (feelers).

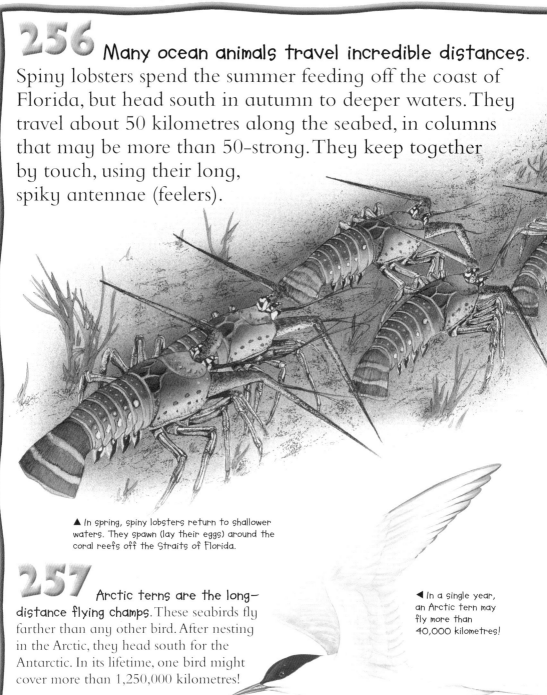

▲ In spring, spiny lobsters return to shallower waters. They spawn (lay their eggs) around the coral reefs off the Straits of Florida.

257 Arctic terns are the long-distance flying champs. These seabirds fly farther than any other bird. After nesting in the Arctic, they head south for the Antarctic. In its lifetime, one bird might cover more than 1,250,000 kilometres!

◀ In a single year, an Arctic tern may fly more than 40,000 kilometres!

258

Grey whales migrate, or travel, farther than any other mammal. There are two main grey whale populations in the Pacific. One spends summer off the Alaskan coast. In winter they migrate south to Mexico to breed. The whales may swim nearly 20,000 kilometres in a year. The other grey whale group spends summer off the coast of Russia, then travels south to Korea.

► Grey whales spend summer in the Bering Sea, feeding on tiny, shrimp-like creatures called amphipods. They spend their breeding season, December to March, in the warmer waters off Mexico.

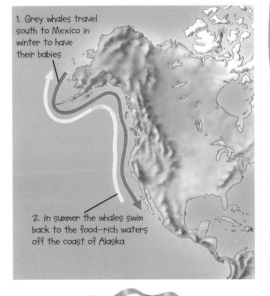

1. Grey whales travel south to Mexico in winter to have their babies

2. In summer the whales swim back to the food-rich waters off the coast of Alaska

259

Baby loggerhead turtles make a two-year journey. They are born on beaches in Japan. The hatchlings hurry down to the sea and set off across the Pacific to Mexico, a journey of 10,000 kilometres. They spend about five years there before returning to Japan to breed.

▼ Not all loggerhead hatchlings make it to the sea. As they race down the beach, some are picked off by hungry gulls or crabs.

I DON'T BELIEVE IT!
Eels and salmon swim thousands of kilometres from the sea to spawn in the same river nurseries where they were born.

On the wing

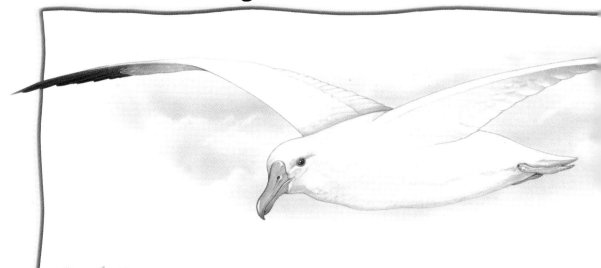

260 **Wandering albatrosses are the biggest seabirds.** An albatross has a wingspan of around three metres – about the length of a family car! These sea birds are so large, they take off by launching from a cliff. Albatrosses spend months at sea. They are such expert gliders that they even sleep on the wing. To feed, they land on the sea, where they sit and catch creatures such as squid.

▶ A gannet dives and captures a fishy meal in its beak.

261 **Gannets wear air–bag shock absorbers.** The gannet's feeding technique is to plummet headfirst into the ocean and catch a fish in its beak. It dives at high-speed and hits the water hard. Luckily, the gannet's head is protected with sacs of air that absorb most of the shock.

SEE THE SEA BIRD!

See if you can match these seabirds to their correct names.

Cormorant Grey headed gull
Black tern

a.   b.   c.

Answers:
a. Black tern, b. Grey headed gull
c. Cormorant

262 **Puffins nest in burrows.**
While many birds jostle for space on a
high cliff ledge, puffins dig a burrow on
the clifftop. Here, they lay a single egg.
Both parents feed the chick for the first
six weeks.

▼ Puffins often scrape
their own burrows, or
they may take over an
abandoned rabbit hole.

263 **Boobies dance to attract
a mate.** There are two types of booby,
blue or red-footed. The dancing draws
attention to the male's colourful feet.
Perhaps this stops the females from
mating with the wrong type of bird.

▼ Boobies are tropical
seabirds that nest in colonies.

264
**Frigate birds puff
up a balloon for
their mate.** Male
frigate birds have a
bright-red pouch on
their throat. They
inflate, or blow up,
the pouch as part of
their display to
attract a female.

▲ A frigate
bird shows off
to its mate.

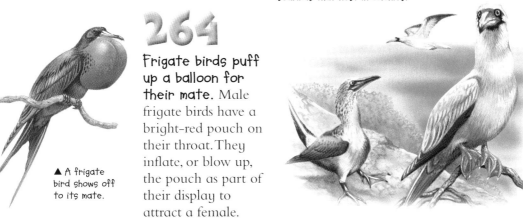

Perfect penguins

265 **Macaroni, chinstrap, jackass and emperor are all types of penguin.** There are 17 different types in total, and most live around the Antarctic. Penguins feed on fish, squid and krill. Their black-and-white plumage is important camouflage. Seen from above, a penguin's black back blends in with the water. The white belly is difficult to distinguish from the sunlit surface of the sea.

Chinstrap penguin

266 **Penguins can swim, but not fly.** They have oily, waterproofed feathers and flipper-like wings. Instead of lightweight, hollow bones – like a flying bird's – some penguins have solid, heavy bones. This enables them to stay underwater longer when diving for food. Emperor penguins can stay under for 15 minutes or more.

I DON'T BELIEVE IT!
The fastest swimming bird is the gentoo penguin. It has been known to swim at speeds of 27 kilometres per hour!

▶ Penguins have a layer of fat under their feathers to protect them in the icy water.

Gentoo penguin

Adélie penguin

King penguin

Emperor penguin

267 **Emperor penguin dads balance an egg on their feet.** They do this to keep their egg off the Antarctic ice, where it would freeze. The female leaves her mate with the egg for the whole two months that it takes to hatch. The male has to go without food during this time. When the chick hatches, the mother returns and both parents help to raise it.

▲ An Adélie penguin builds its nest from stones and small rocks.

268 **Some penguins build stone circles.** This is the way that Adélie and gentoo penguins build nests on the shingled shores where they breed. First, they scrape out a small dip with their flippered feet and then they surround the hollow with a circle of pebbles.

▶ A downy emperor penguin chick cannot find its own food in the sea. It must wait until it has grown its waterproof, adult plumage.

Harvests from the sea

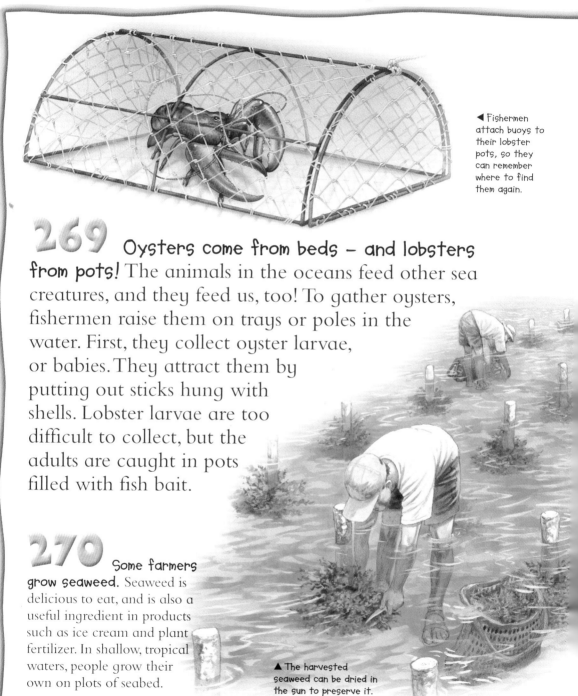

◀ Fishermen attach buoys to their lobster pots, so they can remember where to find them again.

269 **Oysters come from beds – and lobsters from pots!** The animals in the oceans feed other sea creatures, and they feed us, too! To gather oysters, fishermen raise them on trays or poles in the water. First, they collect oyster larvae, or babies. They attract them by putting out sticks hung with shells. Lobster larvae are too difficult to collect, but the adults are caught in pots filled with fish bait.

270 **Some farmers grow seaweed.** Seaweed is delicious to eat, and is also a useful ingredient in products such as ice cream and plant fertilizer. In shallow, tropical waters, people grow their own on plots of seabed.

▲ The harvested seaweed can be dried in the sun to preserve it.

▶ The oil platform's welded–steel legs rest on the seabed. They support the platform around 15 metres above the surface of the water.

Derrick

Crane

Helicopter landing pad

Flare

271 **Sea minerals are big business.** Minerals are useful substances that we mine from the ground – and oceans are full of them! The most valuable are oil and gas, which are pumped from the seabed and piped ashore or transported in huge supertankers. Salt is another important mineral. In hot, low-lying areas, people build walls to hold shallow pools of sea water. The water dries up in the sun, leaving behind crystals of salt.

Oil processing area

272 **There are gemstones under the sea.** Pearls are made by oysters. If a grain of sand is lodged inside an oyster's shell, it irritates its soft body. The oyster coats the sand with a substance called nacre, which is also used to line the inside of the shell. Over the years, more nacre builds up and the pearl gets bigger.

QUIZ
1. What are the young of lobster called?
2. What substances are pumped from the seabed?
3. Is seaweed edible?
4. Which gemstone is made by oysters?

Answers:
1. Larvae 2. Oil and gas
3. Yes 4. Pearl

▶ Pearl divers carry an oyster knife for prising open the oyster's shell.

First voyages

273 The first boats were made from tree trunks. Early people hollowed out tree trunks to craft their own dug-outs. For several hundred years, the Maori peoples of New Zealand made log war canoes, decorating them with beautiful carvings.

▶ Viking longboats were clinker-built, which means that they were made of overlapping planks of wood.

▼ Maori war canoes were usually carved out of kauri pine trunks.

▶ A painted eye on the trireme's hull was believed to protect the boat from evil spirits.

274 Greek warships were oar-some! The ancient Greeks used people-power and sails to move their ships through the water. Triremes were warships rowed by three layers of oarsmen. In battle, the trireme was steered straight at an enemy ship like a battering ram.

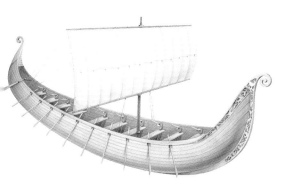

277 **Boats found the way to a new world.** The 1400s were an amazing time of exploration and discovery. One explorer, Christopher Columbus, set sail from Spain in 1492 with a fleet of three ships. He hoped to find a new trade route to India, but instead he found the Americas! Before then, they were not even on the map!

▶ Columbus's fleet consisted of the *Niña*, the *Pinta* and the *Santa Maria*.

275 **Dragons guarded Viking longboats.** Scandinavian seafarers decorated their boats' prows with carvings of dragons and serpents to terrify their enemies. Built from overlapping planks, Viking longboats were very seaworthy. Leif Ericson was the first Viking to cross the Atlantic Ocean to Newfoundland, in North America just over 1000 years ago.

276 **It is thought that Chinese navigators made the first compass–like device about 2500 years ago.** Compasses use the Earth's magnetism to show the directions of north, south, east and west. They are used at sea, where there are no landmarks. The navigators used lodestone, a magnetic rock, to magnetize the needle.

▶ Early compasses were very simple. During the 1300s compasses became more detailed.

BOAT SCRAMBLE!
Unscramble the letters to find the names of six different types of boat.

1. leacvar 2. chenroos
3. rarlewt 4. coclear
5. leglay 6. pecpril

Answers:
1. Caravel 2. Schooner
3. Trawler 4. Coracle
5. Galley 6. Clipper

Pirates!

278 **Pirates once ruled the high seas.** Pirates are sailors who attack and board other ships to steal their cargoes. Their golden age was during the 1600s and 1700s. This was when heavily laden ships carried treasures, weapons and goods back to Europe from colonies in the Americas, Africa and Asia. Edward Teach, better known as Blackbeard, was one of the most terrifying pirates. He attacked ships off the coast of North America during the early 1700s. To frighten his victims, it is said that he used to set fire to his own beard!

▼ Pirate weapons had often been stolen on previous raids. The men fought to the death.

279 **There were women pirates, too.** Piracy was a man's world, but some women also took to the high seas. Mary Read and Anne Bonny were part of a pirate crew sailing around the Caribbean. They wore men's clothes and used fighting weapons, including daggers, cutlasses and pistols.

280

There are still pirates on the oceans. Despite police patrols who watch for pirates and smugglers, a few pirates still operate. Luxury yachts are an easy target and in the South China Sea, pirate gangs on motor boats even attack large merchant ships.

▼ Divers have found some extraordinary hoards of treasure on board sunken galleons.

281

There is treasure lying under the sea. Over the centuries, many ships sunk in storms or hit reefs. They include pirate ships loaded with stolen booty. Some ships were deliberately sunk by pirates. The bed of the Caribbean Sea is littered with the remains of Spanish galleons, many of which still hold treasure!

PIRATE FLAG!

You will need:

paper   paints   brushes

The skull-and-crossbones is the most famous pirate flag, but it was not the only one. Copy one of these designs!

Going under

282 A submarine has dived deeper than 10,000 metres. The two-person *Trieste* made history in 1960 in an expedition to the Mariana Trench in the Pacific, the deepest part of any ocean. It took the submarine five hours to reach the bottom, a distance of 10,911 metres. On the way down, the extreme water pressure cracked part of the craft, but luckily, the two men inside returned to the surface unharmed.

▲ *Trieste* spent 20 minutes at the bottom of the Mariana Trench. The trench is so deep, you could stack the world's tallest building, the CN Tower, inside it 19 times (left)!

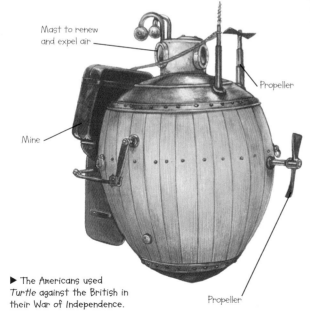

Mast to renew and expel air

Propeller

Mine

▶ The Americans used *Turtle* against the British in their War of Independence.

Propeller

283 The first combat submarine was shaped like an egg! *Turtle* was a one-person submarine that made its test dive in 1776. It was the first real submarine. It did not have an engine – it was driven by a propeller that was turned by hand! *Turtle* was built for war. It travelled just below the surface and could fix bombs to the bottom of enemy ships.

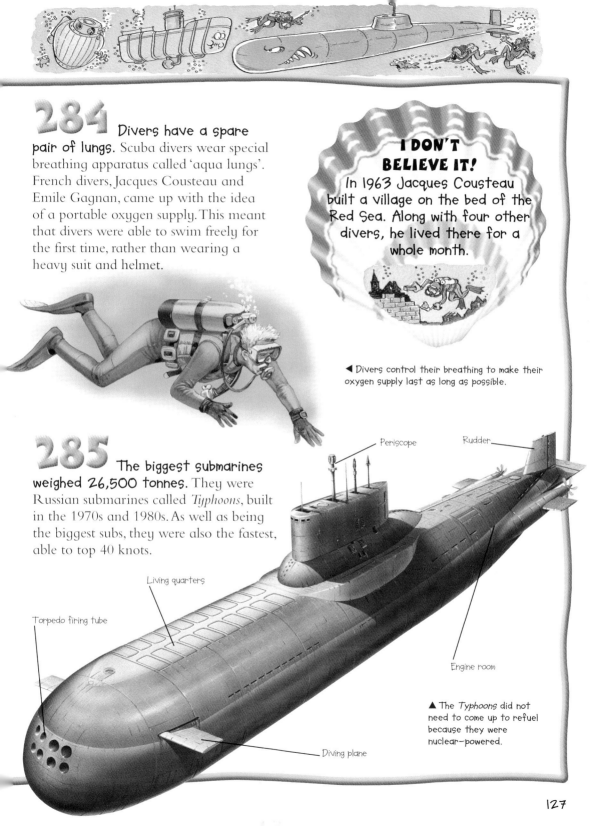

284 Divers have a spare pair of lungs. Scuba divers wear special breathing apparatus called 'aqua lungs'. French divers, Jacques Cousteau and Emile Gagnan, came up with the idea of a portable oxygen supply. This meant that divers were able to swim freely for the first time, rather than wearing a heavy suit and helmet.

I DON'T BELIEVE IT!
In 1963 Jacques Cousteau built a village on the bed of the Red Sea. Along with four other divers, he lived there for a whole month.

◄ Divers control their breathing to make their oxygen supply last as long as possible.

285 The biggest submarines weighed 26,500 tonnes. They were Russian submarines called *Typhoons*, built in the 1970s and 1980s. As well as being the biggest subs, they were also the fastest, able to top 40 knots.

Periscope

Rudder

Living quarters

Torpedo firing tube

Engine room

Diving plane

▲ The *Typhoons* did not need to come up to refuel because they were nuclear-powered.

Superboats

286 **Some ships are invisible.** Stealth warships are not really invisible, of course, but they are hard to detect using radar. There are already materials being used for ships that can absorb some radar signals. Some paints can soak up radar, too, and signals are also bounced off in confusing directions by the ships' strange, angled hulls.

287 **The world's biggest ship is nearly half a kilometre long.** It is a supertanker called *Jahre Viking*. Supertankers carry cargoes of oil around the world. They move slowly because they are so huge and heavy.

▲ An angled, sloping hull gives very little radar echo. This makes the stealth ship's location hard to pinpoint.

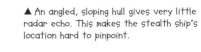

▼ The giant supertanker *Jahre Viking* is just over 458 metres long.

288

Not all boats ride the waves. Hovercrafts sit slightly above the water. They have a rubbery skirt that traps a cushion of air for them to ride on. Without the drag of the water to work against, hovercraft can cross the water much faster.

◀ Hovercraft can travel at up to 65 knots, the equivalent of 120 kilometres per hour.

▼ *Freedom Ship* will be over 1300 metres long. Aircraft 'taxis' will be able to take off and land on its rooftop runway.

289

Ships can give piggy-backs! Heavy-lift ships can sink part of their deck underwater, so a smaller ship can sail aboard for a free ride. Some ships carry planes. Aircraft carriers transport planes that are too small to carry enough fuel for long distances. The deck doubles up as a runway, where the planes take off and land.

290

Freedom Ship will resemble a floating city. It will be one of the first ocean cities, with apartments, shopping centres, a school and a hospital. The people who live on *Freedom* will circle the Earth once every two years. By following the Sun, they will live in constant summertime!

Riding the waves

291 **The first sea sport was surfing.** It took off in the 1950s, but was invented centuries earlier in Hawaii. Hawaii is still one of the best places to surf – at Waimea Bay, surfers catch waves that are up to 11 metres high. The record for the longest rides, though, are made off the coast of Mexico, where it is possible to surf for more than one-and-a-half kilometres.

▶ Modern surfboards are made of super-light materials. This means they create little drag in the water – and the surfer can reach high speeds!

292 **A single boat towed 100 waterskiers!** This record was made off the coast of Australia in 1986 and no one has beaten it yet. The drag boat was a cruiser called *Reef Cat*.

◀ Water skiing is now one of the most popular of all water sports.

QUIZ
1. What was the name of the fastest hydroplane?
2. When did jetskis go on sale?
3. Where is Waimea Bay?
4. What is a trimaran?

Answers:
1. *Spirit of Australia*
2. 1973 3. Hawaii
4. A three-hulled boat

293 **Jetskiers can travel at nearly 100 kilometres per hour.** Jetskis were developed in the 1960s. Their inventor was an American called Clayton Jacobsen who wanted to combine his two favourite hobbies, motorbikes and waterskiing. Today, some jetskiers are professional sportspeople.

◀ Jetskis first went on sale in 1973.

◀ Trimarans have three hulls, while catamarans have two.

294 **Three hulls are sometimes better than one.** Powerboating is an exciting, dangerous sport. Competitors are always trying out new boat designs that will race even faster. Multi-hulled boats minimize drag, but keep the boat steady. Trimarans have three slender, streamlined hulls that cut through the water.

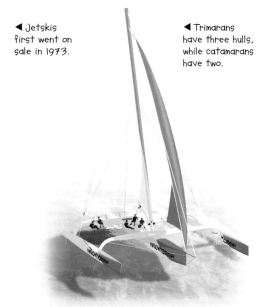

▶ Hydroplanes are motor boats that skim across the surface of the water.

295 **Hydroplanes fly over the waves.** They are a cross between a boat and a plane. Special 'wings' raise the hull two metres above the water. The fastest hydroplane ever was *Spirit of Australia*. Driven by Kenneth Warby, it sped along at more than 500 kilometres per hour above the surface of the water!

Ocean stories

▼ Jason and the Argonauts steer their ship between two huge moving cliffs called the Cyanean Rocks. They faced many dangers on their journey.

296 **The Greek hero Jason made an epic sea voyage.** The ancient Greeks made up lots of sea adventure stories, probably because they lived on scattered islands. In the legend of the Argonauts, a hero called Jason sets off in a boat called the *Argos* with a band of brave men. He goes on a quest to find the Golden Fleece, a precious sheepskin guarded by a fierce dragon.

297 **Neptune (or Poseidon) was an undersea god.** Poseidon was the name used by the ancient Greeks and Neptune by the ancient Romans. Both civilizations pictured their god with a fork called a trident. They blamed their gods for the terrible storms that wrecked boats in the Mediterranean.

▶ Neptune raises his trident and whips up a storm.

▲ The beautiful goddess Aphrodite emerges from the sea.

299
Long ago, people believed in a giant sea monster, called the kraken. The stories were used to explain the dangers of the sea. Sightings of the giant squid might have inspired these tales.

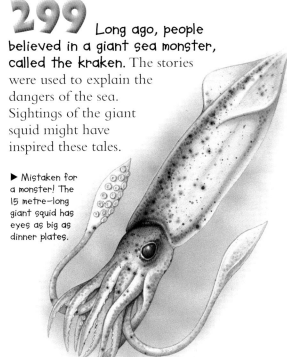

▶ Mistaken for a monster! The 15 metre–long giant squid has eyes as big as dinner plates.

298
The Greek goddess of love was born in the sea. Aphrodite, said to be the daughter of Zeus, was born out of the foam of the sea. The Romans based their love goddess, Venus, on the same story. Lots of artists have painted her rising from the waves in a giant clam shell.

I DON'T BELIEVE IT!
A mermaid's purse is the name given to the eggcases of the dog shark. They look a little bit like handbags!

300
Mermaids lured sailors to their deaths on the rocks. Mythical mermaids were said to be half-woman, half-fish. Folklore tells how the mermaids confused sailors with their beautiful singing – with the result that their ships were wrecked on the rocks.

▼ Mermaids were said to have a fishy tail instead of legs.

What is weather?

301 **Rain, sunshine, snow and storms are all types of weather.** These help us decide what clothes we wear, what food we eat, and what kind of life we lead. Weather also affects how animals and plants survive. Different types of weather are caused by what is happening in the atmosphere, the air above our heads. In some parts of the world, the weather changes every day, in others, it is nearly always the same.

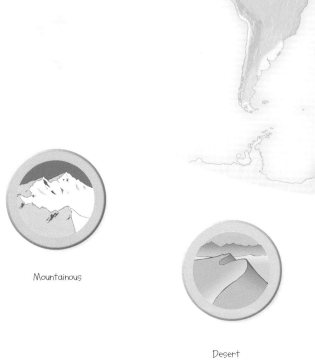

Equator

302 **Tropical, temperate and polar are all types of climate.** Climate is the name we give to patterns of weather over a period of time. Near the Equator, the weather is mostly hot and steamy. We call this a tropical climate. Near the North and South Poles, ice lies on the ground year-round and there are biting-cold blizzards. This is a polar climate. Most of the world has a temperate climate, with a mix of cold and warm seasons.

Mountainous

Desert

North Pole

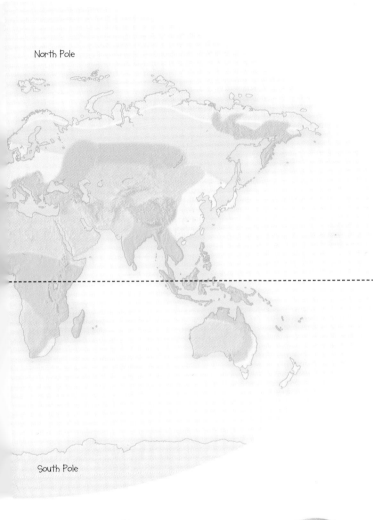

South Pole

Cold temperate

Wet temperate

Dry temperate

Polar

Tropical

▲ Look at the coloured rings to match the different climates scenes to the main map. In general, the warmest climates are found close to the Equator, an imaginary line around the middle of the world. The closer to the Poles, the cooler the climate.

The four seasons

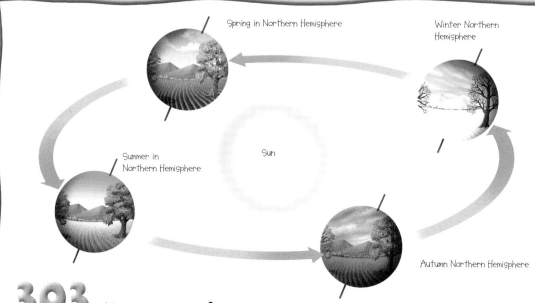

Spring in Northern Hemisphere

Winter Northern Hemisphere

Sun

Summer in Northern Hemisphere

Autumn Northern Hemisphere

303 The reason for the seasons lies in space.

Our planet Earth plots a path through space that takes it around the Sun. This path, or orbit, takes one year. The Earth is tilted, so over the year first one and then the other Pole leans towards the Sun, giving us seasons. In June, for example, the North Pole leans towards the Sun. The Sun heats the northern half of Earth and there is summer.

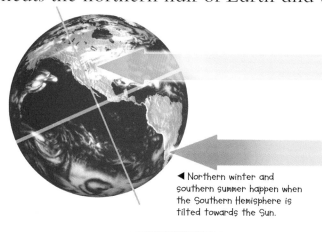

◄ Northern winter and southern summer happen when the Southern Hemisphere is tilted towards the Sun.

304 When it is summer in Argentina, it is winter in Canada. In December, the South Pole leans towards the Sun. Places in the southern half of the world, such as Argentina, have summer. At the same time, places in the northern half, such as Canada, have winter.

305 A day can last 21 hours! Night and day happen because Earth is spinning as it circles the Sun. At the height of summer, places at the North Pole are so tilted towards the Sun that it is light almost all day long. In Stockholm, Sweden, Midsummer's Eve lasts 21 hours because the Sun disappears below the horizon for only three hours.

▲ At the North Pole, the Sun never disappears below the horizon at Midsummer's Day.

▼ Deciduous trees like these lose their leaves in autumn, but evergreens keep their leaves all year round.

I DON'T BELIEVE IT!

When the Sun shines all day in the far north, there is 24-hour night in the far south.

306 Forests change colour in the autumn. Autumn comes between summer and winter. Trees prepare for the winter months ahead by losing their leaves. First, though, they suck back the precious green chlorophyll, or dye, in their leaves, making them turn glorious shades of red, orange and brown.

Fewer seasons

307 Monsoons are winds that carry heavy rains. The rains fall in the tropics in summer during the hot, rainy season. The Sun warms up the sea, which causes huge banks of cloud to form. Monsoons then blow these clouds towards land. Once the rains hit the continent, they can pour for weeks.

▶ When the rains are especially heavy, they cause chaos. Streets turn to rivers and sometimes people's homes are even washed away.

I DON'T BELIEVE IT !

In parts of monsoon India, over 26,000 millimetres of rain have fallen in a single year!

308 Monsoons happen mainly in Asia. However, there are some parts of the Americas close to the Equator that also have a very rainy season. Winds can carry such heavy rain clouds that there are flash floods in the deserts of the southwestern United States. The floods happen because the land has been baked hard during the dry season.

309 Many parts of the tropics have two seasons, not four. They are the parts of the world closest to the Equator, an imaginary line around the middle of the Earth. Here it is always hot, as these places are constantly facing the Sun. However, the movement of the Earth affects the position of a great band of cloud. In June, the tropical areas north of the Equator have the strongest heat and the heaviest rain storms. In December, it is the turn of the areas south of the Equator.

Tropic of Cancer

Equator

Tropic of Capricorn

▲ The tropics lie either side of the Equator, between lines of latitude called the Tropic of Cancer and the Tropic of Capricorn.

310 In a tropical rainforest, you need your umbrella every day! Rainforests have rainy weather all year – but there is still a wet and a dry season. It is just that the wet season is even wetter!

▼ Daily rainfall feeds the lush rainforest vegetation.

What a scorcher!

311 **All our heat comes from the Sun.** The Sun is a star, a super-hot ball of burning gases. It gives off heat rays that travel 150 million kilometres through space to our planet. Over the journey, the rays cool down, but they can still scorch the Earth.

QUIZ

1. How many seasons are there in the tropics?
2. On which continent do most monsoons occur?
3. Where is the hottest recorded place in the world?
4. Is El Niño a wind or a current?

Answers:
1.Two 2.Asia 3.Al Aziziyah in Libya 4.A current

312 **The Sahara is the sunniest place.** This North African desert once had 4300 hours of sunshine in a year! People who live there, such as the Tuareg Arabs, cover their skin to avoid being sunburnt.

313 **The hottest place on Earth is Al Aziziyah in Libya.** It is 58°C in the shade – hot enough to fry an egg!

▶ Desert peoples wear headdresses to protect their skin and eyes from the sun and sand.

▼ A mirage is just a trick of the light. It can make us see something that is not really there.

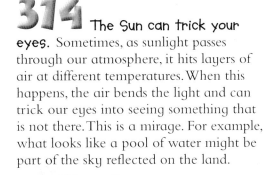

314 **The Sun can trick your eyes.** Sometimes, as sunlight passes through our atmosphere, it hits layers of air at different temperatures. When this happens, the air bends the light and can trick our eyes into seeing something that is not there. This is a mirage. For example, what looks like a pool of water might be part of the sky reflected on the land.

315 **Too much sun brings drought.** Clear skies and sunshine are not always good news. Without rain crops wither, and people and their animals go hungry.

316 **One terrible drought made a 'Dust Bowl'.** Settlers in the American Mid-West were ruined by a long drought during the 1930s. As crops died, there were no roots to hold the soil together. The dry earth turned to dust and some farms simply blew away!

▶ The 'Dust Bowl' was caused by strong winds and dust storms. These destroyed huge areas of land.

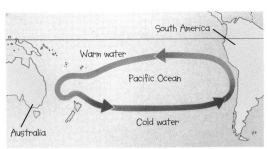

South America

Warm water

Pacific Ocean

Cold water

Australia

317 **A sea current can set forests alight.** All sorts of things affect our weather and climate. The movements of a sea current called El Niño have been blamed for causing terrible droughts – which led to unstoppable forest fires.

◀ El Niño has been known to cause violent weather conditions. It returns on average every four years.

Our atmosphere

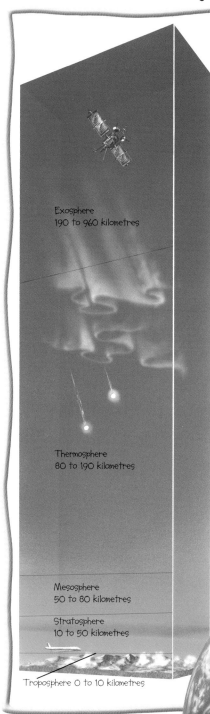

Exosphere
190 to 960 kilometres

Thermosphere
80 to 190 kilometres

Mesosphere
50 to 80 kilometres

Stratosphere
10 to 50 kilometres

Troposphere 0 to 10 kilometres

318 **Our planet is wrapped in a blanket of air.** We call this blanket the atmosphere. It stretches hundreds of kilometres above our heads. The blanket keeps in heat, especially at night when part of the planet faces away from the Sun. During the day, the blanket becomes a sunscreen instead. Without an atmosphere, there would be no weather.

319 **Most weather happens in the troposphere.** This is the layer of atmosphere that stretches from the ground to around 10 kilometres above your head. The higher in the troposphere you go, the cooler the air. Because of this, clouds are most likely to form here. Clouds with flattened tops show just where the troposphere meets the next layer, the stratosphere.

◄ The atmosphere stretches right into space. Scientists have split it into five layers, or spheres, such as the troposphere.

▼ The Earth is surrounded by the atmosphere. It acts as a blanket, protecting us from the Sun's fierce rays.

320 Air just cannot keep still.

Tiny particles in air, called molecules, are always bumping into each other! The more they smash into each other, the greater the air pressure. Generally, there are more smashes lower in the troposphere, because the pull of gravity makes the molecules fall towards the Earth's surface. The higher you go, the lower the air pressure, and the less oxygen there is in the air.

▶ At high altitudes there is less oxygen. That is why mountaineers often wear breathing equipment.

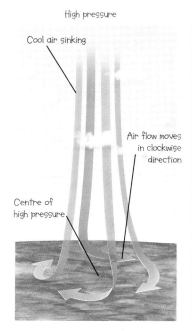

High pressure

Cool air sinking

Air flow moves in clockwise direction

Centre of high pressure

Low pressure

Warm air rising

Air flow moves in anticlockwise direction

Centre of low pressure

321 Warmth makes air move.

When heat from the Sun warms the molecules in air, they move faster and spread out more. This makes the air lighter, so it rises in the sky, creating low pressure. As it gets higher, the air cools. The molecules slow down and become heavier again, so they start to sink back to Earth.

◀ A high pressure weather system gives us warmer weather, while low pressure gives us cooler more unsettled weather.

143

Clouds and rain

322 **Rain comes from the sea.** As the Sun heats the surface of the ocean, some seawater turns into water vapour and rises into the air. As it rises, it cools and turns back into water droplets. Lots of water droplets make clouds. The droplets join together to make bigger and bigger drops that eventually fall as rain. Some rain is soaked up by the land, but a lot finds its way back to the sea. This is called the water cycle.

▶ The water cycle involves all the water on Earth. Water vapour rises from lakes, rivers and the sea to form clouds in the atmosphere.

RAIN GAUGE
You will need:
jam jar waterproof marker pen
ruler notebook pen
Put the jar outside. At the same time each day, mark the rainwater level on the jar with your pen. At the end of a week, empty the jar. Measure and record how much rain fell each day and over the whole week.

323 **Some mountains are so tall that their summits (peaks) are hidden by cloud.** Really huge mountains even affect the weather. When moving air hits a mountain slope it is forced upwards. As it travels up, the temperature drops, and clouds form.

◀ Warm, rising air may be forced up the side of a mountain. At a certain level, lower temperatures make the water form into clouds.

Rain falls, filling rivers

Water is given off by forests

Clouds form

Water evaporates from the sea

The rivers run back to the sea, and the cycle starts again

▼ Virga happens when rain reaches a layer of dry air. The rain droplets turn back into water vapour in mid-air, and seem to disappear.

324 **Some rain never reaches the ground.** The raindrops turn back into water vapour because they hit a layer of super-dry air. You can actually see the drops falling like a curtain from the cloud, but the curtain stops in mid-air. This type of weather is called virga.

325 **Clouds gobble up heat and keep the Earth's temperature regular.** From each 2-metre-square patch of land, clouds can remove the equivalent energy created by a 60-Watt lightbulb.

145

Not just fluffy

326 Clouds come in all shapes and sizes. To help recognize them, scientists split them into ten basic types. The type depends on what the cloud looks like and where it forms in the sky. Cirrus clouds look like wisps of smoke. They form high in the troposphere and rarely mean rain. Stratus clouds form in flat layers and may produce drizzle or a sprinkling of snow. All types of cumulus clouds bring rain. Some are huge cauliflower shapes. They look soft and fluffy – but would feel soggy to touch.

Cumulonimbus clouds give heavy rain showers

▶ The main classes of cloud – cirrus, cumulus and stratus – were named in the 1800s. An amateur British weather scientist called Luke Howard identified the different types.

327 Not all clouds produce rain. Cumulus humilis clouds are the smallest heap-shaped clouds. In the sky, they look like lumpy, cotton wool sausages! They are too small to produce rain but they can grow into much bigger, rain-carrying cumulus clouds. The biggest cumulus clouds, cumulus congestus, bring heavy showers.

Cumulus clouds bring rain

Cirrus clouds occur at great heights from the ground

Cirrostratus

Contrails are the white streaks created by planes

328
Sometimes the sky is filled with white patches of cloud that look like shimmering fish scales. These are called mackerel skies. It takes lots of gusty wind to break the cloud into these little patches, and so mackerel skies are usually a sign of changeable weather.

329
Not all clouds are made by nature. Contrails are streaky clouds that a plane leaves behind it as it flies. They are made of water vapour that comes from the plane's engines. The second it hits the cold air, the vapour turns into ice crystals, leaving a trail of white snow cloud.

MIX AND MATCH
Can you match the names of these five types of clouds to their meanings?

1. Altostratus   a. heap
2. Cirrus   b. layer
3. Cumulonimbus   c. high + layer
4. Cumulus   d. wisp
5. Stratus   e. heap + rain

Answers:
1. C 2. D 3. E
4. A 5. B

Stratus clouds can bring drizzle or appear as fog

Flood warning

▲ Flooding can cause great damage to buildings and the countryside.

330 **Too much rain brings floods.** There are two different types of floods. Flash floods happen after a short burst of heavy rainfall, usually caused by thunderstorms. Broadscale flooding happens when rain falls steadily over a wide area – for weeks or months – without stopping. When this happens, rivers slowly fill and eventually burst their banks. Tropical storms, such as hurricanes, can also lead to broadscale flooding.

331 **There can be floods in the desert.** When a lot of rain falls very quickly on to land that has been baked dry, it cannot soak in. Instead, it sits on the surface, causing flash floods.

◀ A desert flash flood can create streams of muddy brown water. After the water level falls, vegetation bursts into life.

332 **There really was a Great Flood.** The Bible tells of a terrible flood, and how a man called Noah was saved. Recently, explorers found the first real evidence of the Flood – a sunken beach 140 metres below the surface of the Black Sea. There are ruins of houses, dating back to 5600BC. Stories of a huge flood in ancient times do not appear only in the Bible – the Babylonians and Greeks told of one, too.

▲ In the Bible story, Noah survived the Great Flood by building a huge wooden boat called an ark.

333 **Mud can flood.** When rain mixes with earth it makes mud. On bare mountainsides, there are no tree roots to hold the soil together. An avalanche of mud can slide off the mountain. The worst-ever mudslide happened after flooding in Colombia, South America in 1985. It buried 23,000 people from the town of Armero.

▼ Mudslides can devastate whole towns and villages, as the flow of mud covers everything it meets.

I DON'T BELIEVE IT!

The ancient Egyptians had a story to explain the yearly flooding of the Nile. They said the goddess Isis filled the river with tears, as she cried for her lost husband.

Deep freeze

334 Snow is made of tiny ice crystals. When air temperatures are very cold – around 0°C – the water droplets in the clouds freeze to make tiny ice crystals. Sometimes, individual crystals fall, but usually they clump together into snowflakes.

335 No two snowflakes are the same. This is because snowflakes are made up of ice crystals, and every ice crystal is as unique as your fingerprint. Most crystals look like six-pointed stars, but they come in other shapes too.

▲ Falling snow is made worse by strong winds, which can form deep drifts.

▶ Ice crystals seen under a microscope. A snowflake that is several centimetres across will be made up of lots of crystals like these.

▶ An avalanche gathers speed as it thunders down the mountainside.

338 Avalanches are like giant snowballs. They happen after lots of snow falls on a mountain. The slightest movement or sudden noise can jolt the pile of snow and start it moving down the slope. As it crashes down, the avalanche picks up extra snow and can end up large enough to bury whole towns.

339 Marksmen shoot at snowy mountains. One way to prevent deadly avalanches is to stop too much snow from building up. In mountain areas, marksmen set off mini avalanches on purpose. They make sure people are out of the danger zone, then fire guns to trigger a snowslide.

336 Ice can stay frozen for millions of years. At the North and South Poles, the weather never warms up enough for the ice to thaw. When fresh snow falls, it presses down on the snow already there, forming thick sheets. Some ice may not have melted for a million years or more.

337 Black ice is not really black. Drizzle or rain turns to ice when it touches freezing-cold ground. This 'black' ice is see-through, and hard to spot against a road's dark tarmac. It is also terribly slippery – like a deadly ice rink.

▲ Antarctica is a frozen wilderness. The ice piles up to form amazing shapes, like this arch.

When the wind blows

340 **Wind is moving air.** Winds blow because air is constantly moving from areas of high pressure to areas of low pressure. The bigger the difference in temperature between the two areas, the faster the wind blows.

▶ These trees have been forced into strange shapes by the wind.

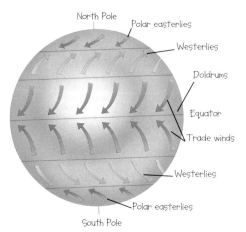

North Pole
Polar easterlies
Westerlies
Doldrums
Equator
Trade winds
Westerlies
Polar easterlies
South Pole

▲ This map shows the pattern of the world's main winds.

341 **Trade winds blow one way north of the Equator, and another way in the south.** Trade winds blow in the tropics, where air is moving to an area of low pressure at the Equator. Their name comes from their importance to traders, when goods travelled by sailing ship.

342 **Winds have names.** World wind patterns are called global winds. The most famous are the trade winds that blow towards the Equator. There are also well-known local winds, such as the cold, dry mistral that blows down to southern France, or the hot, dry sirroco that blows north of the Sahara.

QUIZ

1. At what temperature does water freeze?
2. What does the Beaufort Scale measure?
3. What are the mistral and sirroco?
4. How many sides does an ice crystal usually have?

Answers:
1. 0°C
2. Wind strength
3. Local winds 4. Six

343

You can tell how windy it is by looking at the leaves on a tree. Wind ranges from light breezes to hurricanes. Its strength is measured on the Beaufort Scale, named after the Irish admiral who devised it. The scale ranges from Force 0, meaning total calm, to Force 12, which is a hurricane

▶ The Beaufort Scale.

Force 0: Calm

Force 1: Light air

Force 2: Light breeze

Force 3: Gentle breeze

Force 4: Moderate breeze

Force 5: Fresh breeze

Force 6: Strong breeze

Force 7: Near gale

Force 8: Gale

Force 9: Strong gale

Force 10: Storm

Force 11: Violent storm

Force 12: Hurricane

344

Wind can turn on your TV. People can harness the energy of the wind to make electricity for our homes. Tall turbines are positioned in windy spots. As the wind turns the turbine, the movement powers a generator and produces electrical energy.

345

Wind can make you mad! The Föhn wind, which blows across Switzerland, Austria and Bavaria in southern Germany, brings with it changeable weather. This has been blamed for road accidents and even bouts of madness!

Thunderbolts and lightning

346 **Thunderstorms are most likely in summer.** Hot weather creates warm, moist air that rises and forms towering cumulonimbus clouds. Inside each cloud, water droplets and ice crystals bang about, building up positive and negative electrical charges. Electricity flows between the charges, creating a flash that heats the air around it. Lightning is so hot that it makes the air expand, making a loud noise or thunderclap. Cloud-to-cloud lightning is called sheet lightning, while lightning travelling from the cloud to the ground is called fork lightning.

347 Lightning comes in different colours. If there is rain in the thundercloud, the lightning looks red; if there's hail, it looks blue. Lightning can also be yellow or white.

▼ Lightning conductors absorb the shock and protect tall buildings.

▶ Dramatic lightning flashes light up the sky.

348 Tall buildings are protected from lightning. Church steeples and other tall structures are often struck by bolts of lightning. This could damage the building, or give electric shocks to people inside, so lightning conductors are placed on the roof. These channel the lightning safely away.

HOW CLOSE?
Lightning and thunder happen at the same time, but light travels faster than sound. Count the seconds between the flash and the clap and divide them by three. This is how many kilometres away the storm is.

349 A person can survive a lightning strike. Lightning is very dangerous and can give a big enough shock to kill you. However, an American park ranger called Roy Sullivan survived being struck seven times.

▼ A sudden hail storm can leave the ground littered with small chunks of ice.

350 Hailstones can be as big as melons! These chunks of ice can fall from thunderclouds. The biggest ever fell in Gopaljang, Bangladesh, in 1986 and weighed 1 kilogram each!

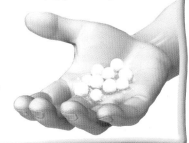

Eye of the hurricane

351 **Some winds travel at speeds of more than 120 kilometres per hour.** Violent tropical storms happen when strong winds blow into an area of low pressure and start spinning very fast. They develop over warm seas and pick up speed until they reach land, where there is no more moist sea air to feed them. Such storms bring torrential rain.

352 **The centre of a hurricane is calm and still.** This part is called the 'eye'. As the eye of the storm passes over, there is a pause in the rains and wind.

I DON'T BELIEVE IT !

Tropical storms are called different names. Hurricanes develop over the Atlantic, typhoons over the Pacific, and cyclones over the Indian Ocean.

▼ This satellite photograph of a hurricane shows how the storm whirls around a central, still 'eye'.

▶ A Hurricane Hunter heads into the storm.

353 **Hurricane Hunters fly close to the eye of a hurricane.** These are special weather planes that fly into the storm in order to take measurements. It is a dangerous job for the pilots, but the information they gather helps to predict the hurricane's path – and saves lives.

354 Hurricanes have names.

One of the worst hurricanes was Hurricane Andrew, which battered the coast of Florida in 1992. Perhaps there is a hurricane named after you!

▲ A hurricane brings battering rain and massive waves.

355 Hurricanes whip up wild waves.

As the storm races over the ocean, the winds create giant waves. These hit the shore as a huge sea surge. In 1961, the sea surge following Hurricane Hattie washed away Belize City in South America.

356 Typhoons saved the Japanese from Genghis Khan.

The 13th-century Mongol leader made two attempts to invade Japan – and both times, a terrible typhoon battered his fleet and saved the Japanese!

▶ A typhoon prevented Genghis Khan's navy from invading Japan.

Wild whirling winds

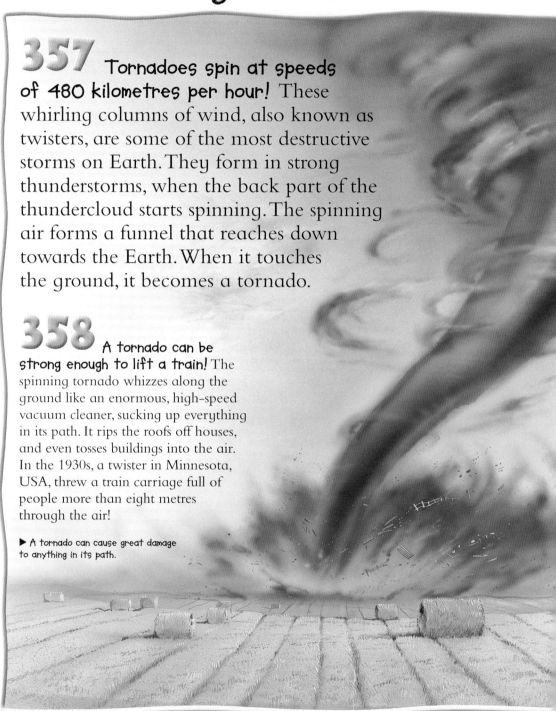

357 **Tornadoes spin at speeds of 480 kilometres per hour!** These whirling columns of wind, also known as twisters, are some of the most destructive storms on Earth. They form in strong thunderstorms, when the back part of the thundercloud starts spinning. The spinning air forms a funnel that reaches down towards the Earth. When it touches the ground, it becomes a tornado.

358 **A tornado can be strong enough to lift a train!** The spinning tornado whizzes along the ground like an enormous, high-speed vacuum cleaner, sucking up everything in its path. It rips the roofs off houses, and even tosses buildings into the air. In the 1930s, a twister in Minnesota, USA, threw a train carriage full of people more than eight metres through the air!

▶ A tornado can cause great damage to anything in its path.

359 Tornado Alley is a twister hotspot in the American Mid-West.

This is where hot air travelling north from the Gulf of Mexico meets cold polar winds travelling south, and creates huge thunderclouds. Of course, tornadoes can happen anywhere in the world when the conditions are right.

▲ The shaded area shows Tornado Alley, where there are hundreds of tornadoes each year.

360 A pillar of whirling water can rise out of a lake or the sea.

Waterspouts are spiralling columns of water that can be sucked up by a tornado as it forms over a lake or the sea. They tend to spin more slowly than tornadoes, because water is much heavier than air.

▲ Waterspouts can suck up fish living in a lake!

I DON'T BELIEVE IT !

Loch Ness in Scotland is famous for sightings of a monster nicknamed Nessie. Perhaps people who have seen Nessie were really seeing a waterspout.

361 Dust devils are desert tornadoes.

They shift tonnes of sand and cause terrible damage – they can strip the paintwork from a car in seconds!

▶ A whirling storm of sand in the desert.

Pretty lights

362 **Rainbows are made up of seven colours.** They are caused by sunlight passing through falling raindrops. The water acts like a glass prism, splitting the light. White light is made up of seven colours – red, orange, yellow, green, blue, indigo and violet – so these are the colours, from top to bottom, that make up the rainbow.

REMEMBER IT!

Richard Of York Gave Battle In Vain

The first letter of every word of this rhyme gives the first letter of each colour of the rainbow – as it appears in the sky:

Red Orange Yellow Green Blue Indigo Violet

363 **Two rainbows can appear at once.** The top rainbow is a reflection of the bottom one, so its colours appear the opposite way round, with the violet band at the top and red at the bottom.

364 **Some rainbows appear at night.** They happen when falling raindrops split moonlight, rather than sunlight. This sort of rainbow is called a moonbow.

▲ Although a fogbow is colourless, its inner edge may appear slightly blue and its outer edge slightly red.

365 *It is not just angels that wear halos!* When you look at the Sun or Moon through a curtain of ice crystals, they seem to be surrounded by a glowing ring of light called a halo.

366 Three suns can appear in our sky! 'Mock suns' are two bright spots that appear on either side of the Sun. They often happen at the same time as a halo, and have the same cause – light passing through ice crystals in the air.

▼ An aurora – the most dazzling natural light show on Earth!

▶ Mock suns are also known as parhelia or sundogs.

367 Some rainbows are just white. Fogbows happen when sunlight passes through a patch of fog. The water droplets in the fog are too small to work like prisms, so the arching bow is white or colourless.

▲ A halo looks like a circle of light surrounding the Sun or Moon.

368 Auroras are curtains of lights in the sky. They happen in the far north or south of the world when particles from the Sun smash into molecules in the air – at speeds of 1600 kilometres per hour. The lights may be blue, red or yellow.

Made for weather

369 Camels can go for two weeks without a drink. These animals are adapted to life in a hot, dry climate. They do not sweat until their body temperature hits 40°C, which helps them to save water. The humps on their backs are fat stores, which are used for energy when food and drink is scarce.

370 Lizards lose salt through their noses. Most animals get rid of excess salt in their urine, but lizards, such as iguanas and geckos, live in dry parts of the world. They need to lose as little water from their bodies as possible.

Camel

371 Even toads can survive in the desert. The spadefoot toad copes with desert conditions by staying underground in a burrow for most of the year. It only comes to the surface after a shower of rain.

Iguana

Banded gecko

▶ Beneath its gleaming—white fur, the polar bear's skin is black to absorb heat from the Sun.

372 Polar bears have black skin.

These bears have all sorts of special ways to survive the polar climate. Plenty of body fat and thick fur keeps them snug and warm, while their black skin soaks up as much warmth from the Sun as possible.

373 Acorn woodpeckers store nuts for winter.

Animals in temperate climates have to be prepared if they are to survive the cold winter months. Acorn woodpeckers turn tree trunks into larders. During autumn, when acorns are ripe, the birds collect as many as they can, storing them in holes that they bore into a tree.

▶ Storing acorns helps this woodpecker survive the cold winter months.

◀ These animals have adapted to life in very dry climates. However, they live in different deserts around the world.

Spadefoot toad

Weather myths

374 **People once thought the Sun was a god.** The sun god was often considered to be the most important god of all, because he brought light and warmth and ripened crops. The ancient Egyptians built pyramids that pointed up to their sun god, Re, while the Aztecs believed that their sun god, Huitzilpochtli, had even shown them where to build their capital city.

375 **The Vikings thought a god brought thunder.** Thor was the god of war and thunder, worshipped across what is now Scandinavia. The Vikings pictured Thor as a red-bearded giant. He carried a hammer that produced bolts of lightning. Our day, Thursday, is named in Thor's honour.

◀ In Scandinavian mythology, Thor was the god of thunder.

▲ The Egyptian sun god, Re, was often shown with the head of a falcon.

376 **Hurricanes are named after a god.** The Mayan people lived in Central America, the part of the world that is most affected by hurricanes. Their creator god was called Huracan.

377 Totem poles honoured the Thunderbird.

Certain tribes of Native American Indians built tall, painted totem poles, carved in the image of the Thunderbird. They wanted to keep the spirit happy, because they thought it brought rain to feed the plants.

▶ A Native American Indian totem pole depicting the spirit of the Thunderbird.

378 People once danced for rain.

In hot places such as Africa, people developed dances to bring rain. These were performed by the village shaman (religious woman or man), using wooden instruments such as bullroarers. Sometimes water was sprinkled on the ground. Rain dances are still performed in some countries today.

◀ Shamans wore a special costume for their rain dance.

MAKE A BULLROARER

You will need:

a wooden ruler   some string

Ask an adult to drill a hole in one end of the ruler. Thread through the string, and knot it, to stop it slipping through the hole. In an open space, whirl the instrument above your head to create a wind noise!

Rain or shine?

379 **Seaweed can tell us if rain is on the way.** Long ago, people looked to nature for weather clues. One traditional way of forecasting was to hang up strands of seaweed. If the seaweed stayed slimy, the air was damp and rain was likely. If the seaweed shrivelled up, the weather would be dry.

▲ Kelp picks up any moisture in the air, so it is a good way of telling how damp the atmosphere is.

I DON'T BELIEVE IT!

People used to say that cows lay down when rain was coming – but there is no truth in it! They lie down whether rain is on the way or not!

380 **'Red sky at night is the sailor's delight'.** This is one of the most famous pieces of weather lore and means that a glorious sunset is followed by a fine morning. The saying is also known as 'shepherd's delight'. There is no evidence that the saying is true, though.

381 **Groundhogs tell the weather when they wake.** Of course, they don't really, but in parts of the USA, Groundhog Day is a huge celebration. On 2 February, people gather to see the groundhog come out. If you see the creature's shadow, it means there are six more weeks of cold to come.

▼ A blood-red sunset is delightful to look at, but it can't help a sailor to predict the next day's weather.

▲ The Moon is clearly visible in a cloudless night sky. Its light casts a silvery glow over the Earth.

382 'Clear moon, frost soon'. This old saying does have some truth in it. If there are few clouds in the sky, the view of the Moon will be clear – and there will also be no blanket of cloud to keep in the Earth's heat. That makes a frost more likely – during the colder months, at least.

383 The earliest weather records are over 3000 years old. They were found on a piece of tortoiseshell and had been written down by Chinese weather watchers. The inscriptions describe when it rained or snowed and how windy it was.

◀ Records of ancient weather were scratched on to this piece of shell.

Instruments and inventors

384 The Tower of Winds was built 2000 years ago. It was an eight-sided building and is the first known weather station. It had a wind vane on the roof and a water clock inside.

▲ This is how the Tower of Winds looks today. It was built by Andronicus of Cyrrhus in Athens around 75BC. Its eight sides face the points of the compass: north, northeast, east, southeast, south, southwest, west and northwest.

385 The first barometer was made by one of Galileo's students. Barometers measure air pressure. The first person to describe air pressure – and to make an instrument for measuring it – was an Italian, Evangelista Torricelli. He had studied under the great scientist Galileo. Torricelli made his barometer in 1643.

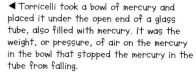

◀ Torricelli took a bowl of mercury and placed it under the open end of a glass tube, also filled with mercury. It was the weight, or pressure, of air on the mercury in the bowl that stopped the mercury in the tube from falling.

386 Weather cocks have a special meaning. They have four pointers that show the directions of north, south, east and west. The cockerel at the top swivels so that its head always shows the direction of the wind.

▶ Weather cocks are often placed on top of church steeples.

387
A weather house really can predict the weather. It is a type of hygrometer – an instrument that detects how much moisture is in the air. If there is lots, the rainy-day character comes out of the door!

▶ Weather houses have two figures. One comes out when the air is damp and the other when the air is dry.

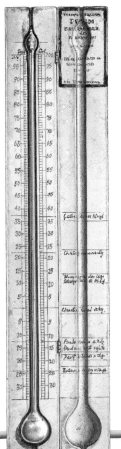

◀ This early thermometer shows both the Fahrenheit and the Celsius temperature scales.

388
Fahrenheit made the first thermometer in 1714. Thermometers are instruments that measure temperature. Gabriel Daniel Fahrenheit invented the thermometer using a blob of mercury sealed in an airtight tube. The Fahrenheit scale for measuring heat was named after him. The Centigrade scale was introduced in 1742 by the Swedish scientist Anders Celsius.

QUIZ
1. What is another name for the liquid metal, mercury?
2. What does an anemometer measure?
3. What does a wind vane measure?
4. On the Fahrenheit scale, at what temperature does water freeze?

Answers:
1. Quicksilver 2. Wind speed 3. Wind direction 4. 32°F

World of weather

389 **Working out what the weather will be like is called forecasting.** By looking at changes in the atmosphere, and comparing them to weather patterns of the past, forecasters can make an accurate guess at what the weather will be tomorrow, the next day, or even further ahead. But even forecasters get it wrong sometimes!

390 **The first national weather offices appeared in the 1800s.** This was when people realized that science could explain how weather worked – and save people from disasters. The first network of weather stations was set up in France, in 1855. This was after the scientist Le Verrier showed how a French warship, sunk in a storm, could have been saved. Le Verrier explained how the path of the storm could have been tracked, and the ship sailed to safety.

A cold front is shown by a blue triangle

A warm front is shown by a red semi-circle

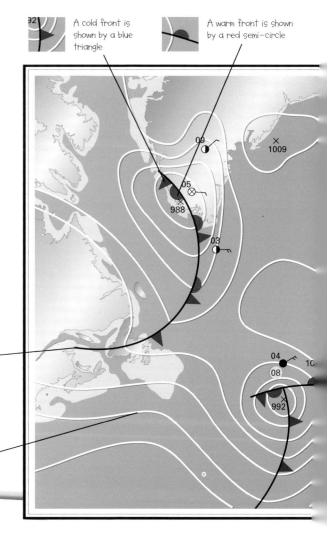

Look for the black lines with red semi-circles and blue triangles – they represent an occluded front, where a cold front meets a warm front

These white lines are isobars – they connect places where air pressure is the same

WEATHER SYMBOLS

Learn how to represent the weather on your own synoptic charts. Here are some of the basic symbols to get you started. You may come across them in newspapers or while watching television. Can you guess what they mean?

391 Nations need to share weather data. By 1865, nearly 60 weather stations across Europe were swapping information. These early weather scientists, or meteorologists, realized that they needed to present their information using symbols that they could all understand. To this day, meteorologists plot their findings on maps called synoptic charts. They use lines called isobars to show which areas have the same air pressure. The Internet makes it easier for meteorologists to access information.

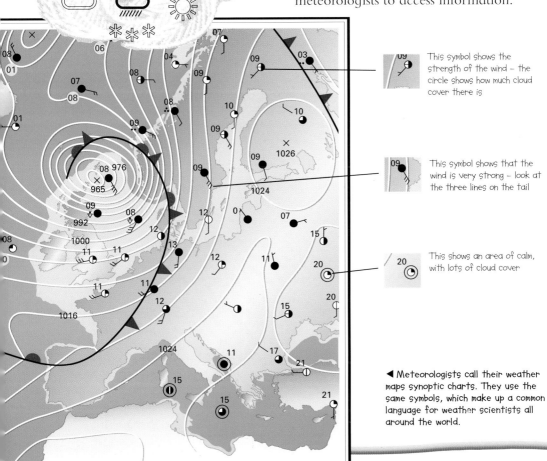

This symbol shows the strength of the wind – the circle shows how much cloud cover there is

This symbol shows that the wind is very strong – look at the three lines on the tail

This shows an area of calm, with lots of cloud cover

◀ Meteorologists call their weather maps synoptic charts. They use the same symbols, which make up a common language for weather scientists all around the world.

Weather watch

392 Balloons can tell us about the weather.
Weather balloons are hot-air balloons that are sent
high into the atmosphere. As they rise, onboard
equipment takes readings. These find out air pressure,
and how moist, or humid, the air is, as well as how
warm. The findings are radioed back
to meteorologists on the ground,
using a system called
radiosonde. Hundreds of
balloons are launched
around the world every day.

▶ A weather balloon carries its scientific
instruments high into the atmosphere.

393 Some planes hound the
weather. Weather planes provide more
atmospheric measurements than balloons
can. *Snoopy* is the name of one of the British
weather planes. The instruments are carried
on its long, pointy nose, so they can test the
air ahead of the plane.

▼ *Snoopy's* long nose carries all the equipment
needed to monitor the weather.

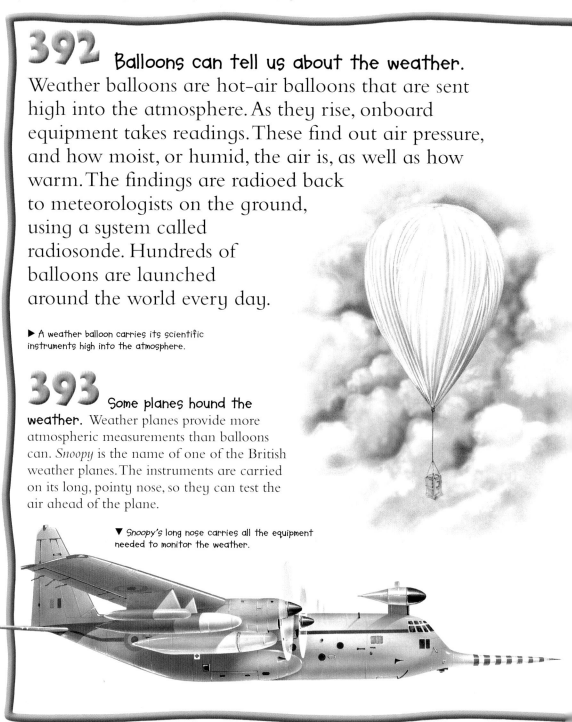

394 Satellites help save lives.

Their birds'-eye view of the Earth allows them to take amazing pictures of our weather systems. They can track hurricanes as they form over the oceans. Satellite-imaging has helped people to leave their homes and get out of a hurricane's path just in time.

I DON'T BELIEVE IT!

Some of the best weather photos have been taken by astronauts in space.

395 Some weather stations

are all at sea. Weather buoys float on the surface of the oceans, measuring air pressure, temperature and wind direction. They are fitted with transmitters that beam information to satellites in space – which bounce the readings on to meteorologists. Tracking the buoys is just as important. They are carried along by ocean currents, which have a huge effect on our weather systems.

▲ A weather satellite takes photographs of Earth's weather systems from space.

▶ Currents carry the floating weather buoys around the oceans.

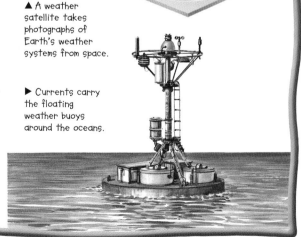

Changing climate

396 Climate change destroyed the dinosaurs – but no one can agree on what caused it. The best explanation is that a huge piece of space rock, called a meteorite, smashed into Earth. It threw up a giant cloud of dust that blocked out the Sun, plunging the world into cold and dark.

▼ Could a meteorite have crashed to Earth and changed the climate? A meteorite crater found in the Gulf of Mexico dates to 65 million years ago – exactly the time that the dinosaurs died out. Perhaps the impact changed the warm climate the dinosaurs were so used to.

▼ Vikings settled on Greenland's coastline. Inland areas were covered in ice.

397 Greenland used to be green! This island lies in the Arctic Ocean and is mostly covered by a huge ice sheet. Even in Viking times, Greenland was cold, but Viking settlers built at least two farming colonies there. These died out around the 1400s, after the climate cooled.

398

A volcano can change the climate! Big volcanic explosions can create dust that blots out the Sun, just as a meteorite impact can. Dust from the 1815 eruption of a volcano called Tambora did this. This made many crops fail around the world and many people starved.

399

Tree–felling is affecting our weather. In areas of Southeast Asia and South America, rainforests are being cleared for farming. When the trees are burned, the fires release carbon dioxide – a greenhouse gas which helps to blanket the Earth and keep in the heat. Unfortunately, high levels of carbon dioxide raise the temperature too much.

◀ Like all plants, rainforest trees take in carbon dioxide and give out oxygen. As rainforests are destroyed, the amount of carbon dioxide in the atmosphere increases.

400

Air temperatures are rising. Scientists think the average world temperature may increase by around 1.5 °C this century. This may not sound like much, but the extra warmth will mean more storms, including hurricanes and tornadoes, and more droughts too.

QUIZ

1. What may have caused the death of the dinosaurs?
2. Which settlers once lived along the coast of Greenland?
3. Which gas do plants take in?

Answers:
1. Meteorite impact 2. Vikings 3. Carbon dioxide

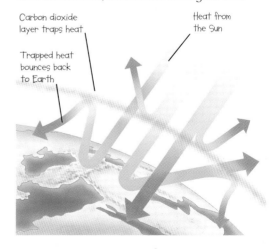

Carbon dioxide layer traps heat

Heat from the Sun

Trapped heat bounces back to Earth

▶ Too much carbon dioxide in the atmosphere creates a 'greenhouse effect'. Just as glass traps heat, so does carbon dioxide. This means more storms and droughts.

Why do we need science?

401 Even one hundred books like this could not explain all the reasons why we need science. Toasters, bicycles, mobile phones, computers, cars, light bulbs – all the gadgets and machines we use every day are the results of scientific discoveries. Houses, skyscrapers, bridges and rockets are built using science. Our knowledge of medicines, nature, light and sound comes from science. Then there is the science of predicting the weather, investigating how stars shine, finding out why carrots are orange…

▶ In a big city, almost every vehicle, building, machine and gadget is based on science and technology.

Machines big and small

402 Machines are everywhere! They help us do things, or make doing them easier. Every time you play on a see-saw, you are using a machine! A lever is a stiff bar that tilts at a point called the pivot or fulcrum. The pivot of the see-saw is in the middle. Using the see-saw as a lever, a small person can lift a big person by sitting further from the pivot.

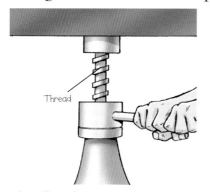

Thread

403 The screw is another simple but useful scientific machine. It is a ridge, or thread, wrapped around a bar or pole. It changes a small turning motion into a powerful pulling or lifting movement. Wood screws hold together furniture or shelves. A car jack lets you lift up a whole car.

▶ On a see-saw lever, the pivot is in the middle. Other levers have pivots at the end.

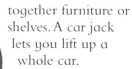

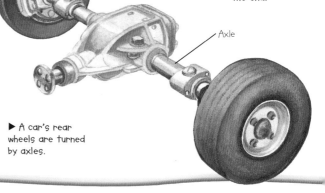

Axle

404 Where would you be without wheels? Not going very far. The wheel is a simple machine, a circular disc that turns around its centre on a bar called an axle. Wheels carry heavy weights easily. There are giant wheels on big trucks and trains and small wheels on rollerblades.

▶ A car's rear wheels are turned by axles.

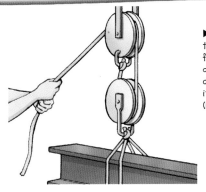

▲ Two pulleys together reduce the force needed to lift a heavy girder by one half.

▶ Gears change the turning direction of a force. They can slow it down or speed it up – and even convert it into a sliding force (rack and pinion).

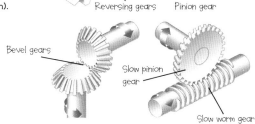

Reversing gears   Pinion gear   Sliding rack

Bevel gears   Slow pinion gear   Slow worm gear

405 A pulley turns around, like a wheel.
It has a groove around its edge for a cable or rope. Lots of pulleys allow us to lift very heavy weights easily. The pulleys on a tower crane can lift huge steel girders to the top of a skyscraper.

406 Gears are like wheels, with pointed teeth around the edges.
They change a fast, weak turning force into a slow, powerful one – or the other way around. On a bicycle, you can pedal up the steepest hill in bottom (lowest) gear, then speed down the other side in top (highest) gear.

Lever

Pivot

I DON'T BELIEVE IT!

A ramp is a simple machine called an inclined plane. It is easier to walk up a ramp than to jump straight to the top.

When science is hot!

407 **Fire! Flames! Burning! Heat!** The science of heat is important in all kinds of ways. Not only do we cook with heat, but we also warm our homes and heat water. Burning happens in all kinds of engines in cars, trucks, planes and rockets. It is also used in factory processes, from making steel to shaping plastics.

408 **Heat moves by conduction.** A hot object will pass on, or transfer, some of its heat to a cooler one. Dip a metal spoon in a hot drink and the spoon handle soon warms up. Heat is conducted from the drink, through the metal.

◀ Metal is a good conductor of heat. Put a teaspoon in a hot drink and feel how quickly it heats up.

▲ A firework burns suddenly as an explosive, with heat, light and sound... BANG!

409 **Heat moves by invisible 'heat rays'.** This is called thermal radiation and the rays are infrared waves. The Sun's warmth radiates through space as infrared waves, to reach Earth.

410 Burning, also called combustion, is a chemical process. Oxygen gas from the air joins to, or combines with, the substance being burned. The chemical change releases lots of heat, and usually light too. If this happens really fast, we call it an explosion.

411 Temperature is the amount of heat in a substance. It is usually measured in degrees Celsius, °C. Water freezes into ice at 0°C, and boils into steam at 100°C. We take temperatures using a device called a thermometer. Your body temperature is probably about 37°C.

▶ A thermometer may be filled with alcohol and red dye. As the temperature goes up, the liquid rises up its tube to show how hot it is. It sinks back down if the temperature falls.

CARRYING HEAT
You will need:

wooden ruler   metal spoon
plastic spatula   heatproof jug
frozen peas   some butter

Find a wooden ruler, a metal spoon and a plastic spatula, all the same length. Fix a frozen pea to one end of each with butter. Put the other ends in a heatproof jug. Ask an adult to fill the jug with hot water. Heat is conducted from the water, up the object, to melt the butter. Which object is the best conductor?

412 Heat moves by convection, especially through liquids and gases. Some of the liquid or gas takes in heat, gets lighter and rises into cooler areas. Then other, cooler, liquid or gas moves in to do the same. You can see this as 'wavy' hot air rising from a flame.

▶ See how hot air shimmers over a candle.

Engine power

413 Imagine having to walk or run everywhere, instead of riding in a car. Engines are machines that use fuel to do work for us and make life easier. Fuel is a substance that has chemical energy stored inside it. The energy is released as heat by burning or exploding the fuel in the engine.

Fan sucks air in

Air is squashed by turbines

Jet fuel is sprayed onto air, and small explosion happens

414 Most cars have petrol engines. A mixture of air and petrol is pushed into a hollow chamber called the cylinder. A spark from a spark plug makes it explode, which pushes a piston down inside the cylinder (see below). This movement is used by gears to turn the wheels. Most cars have four or six cylinders.

415 A diesel engine works in a similar way, but without sparks. The mixture of air and diesel is squashed so much in the cylinder that it becomes hot enough to explode. Diesel engines are used where lots of power is needed, in trucks, diggers, tractors and big trains.

▼ This shows the four-stroke cycle of a petrol engine.

1. Air and petrol mixture is sucked into the cylinder

2. The piston moves up and squeezes the mixture

3. A spark from the plug makes the mixture explode

4. The piston rises to push waste gases out of the cylinder

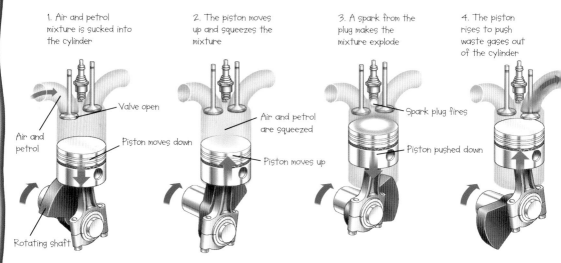

Valve open

Air and petrol

Piston moves down

Air and petrol are squeezed

Piston moves up

Spark plug fires

Piston pushed down

Rotating shaft

▼ Jet engines are very powerful. They use a mixture of air and fuel to push the plane forward at high speed.

Gases roar past exhaust turbines

Hot gases rush out of the engine

Afterburner adds more roaring gases

416 A jet engine mixes air and kerosene and sets fire to it in one long, continuous explosion. Incredibly hot gases blast out of the back of the engine. These push the engine forward – along with the plane.

417 An electric motor passes electricity through coils of wire. This makes the coils magnetic, and they push or pull against magnets around them. The push-pull makes the coils spin on their shaft (axle).

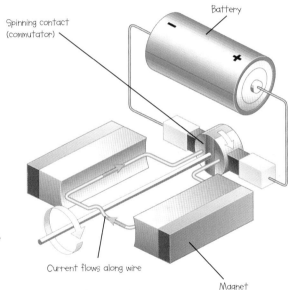

Battery

Spinning contact (commutator)

Current flows along wire

Magnet

418 Engines which burn fuel give out gases and particles through their exhausts. Some of these gases are harmful to the environment. The less we use engines, the better. Electric motors are quiet, efficient and reliable, but they still need fuel – to make the electricity at the power station.

Science on the move

419 Without science, we would have to walk everywhere, or ride a horse. Luckily, scientists and engineers have developed many methods of transport, most importantly, the car. Lots of people can travel together in a bus, train, plane or ship. This uses less energy and resources, and makes less pollution.

Passenger terminal

Underground trains to take passengers to and from the terminal

420 Science is used to stop criminals. Science-based security measures include a 'door frame' that detects metal objects like guns and a scanner which sees inside bags. A sniffer-machine (or dog) can detect the smell of explosives or illegal drugs.

421 Jetways are extending walkways that stretch out like telescopic fingers, right to the plane's doors. Their supports move along on wheeled trolleys driven by electric motors.

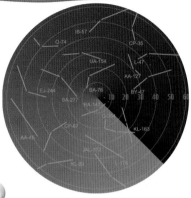

▶ The radar screen shows each aircraft as a blip, with its flight number or identity code.

Jetway

◀ Modern airports are enormous. They can stretch for several miles, and they have a constant flow of planes taking off and landing. Hundreds of people are needed to make sure that everything runs smoothly and on time.

422 Every method of transport needs to be safe and on time. In the airport control tower, air traffic controllers track planes on radar screens. They talk to pilots by radio. Beacons send out radio signals, giving the direction and distance to the airport.

423 On the road, drivers obey traffic lights. On a railway network, train drivers obey similar signal lights of different colours, such as red for stop. Sensors by the track record each train passing and send the information by wires or radio to the control room. Each train's position is shown as a flashing light on a wall map.

▼ Train signals show just two colours – red for stop and green for go.

QUIZ
On traffic lights, what do these colours mean?
1. Green 2. Amber 3. Red 4. Red and amber

Answers:
1. Go 2. Get ready to stop 3. Stop 4. Get ready to go

D-27

Noisy science

424 Listening to the radio or television, playing music, shouting at each other – they all depend on the science of sound – acoustics. Sounds are like invisible waves in the air. The peak (highest point) of the wave is where a region of air is squashed under high pressure. The trough (lowest point) of the wave is a region where air is expanded under low pressure.

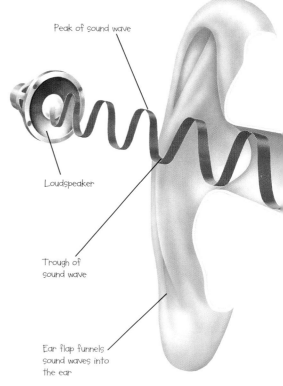

Peak of sound wave

Loudspeaker

Trough of sound wave

Ear flap funnels sound waves into the ear

425 Scientists measure the loudness or intensity of sound in decibels, dB. A very quiet sound like a ticking watch is 10 dB. Ordinary speech is 50–60 dB. Loud music is 90 dB. A jet plane taking off is 120 dB. Too much noise damages the ears.

▲ We cannot see sound waves but we can certainly hear them. They are ripples of high and low pressure in air.

◄ The decibel scale measures the intensity, or energy, in sound.

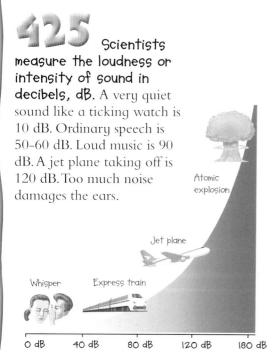

Atomic explosion

Jet plane

Express train

Whisper

O dB   40 dB   80 dB   120 dB   180 dB

426 Whether a sound is high or low is called its pitch, or frequency. It is measured in Hertz, Hz. A singing bird or whining motorcycle has a high pitch. A rumble of thunder or a massive truck has a low pitch. People can hear frequencies from 25 to 20,000 Hz.

428 Sound waves travel about 330 metres every second. This is fast, but it is one million times slower than light waves. Sound waves also bounce off hard, flat surfaces. This is called reflection. The returning waves are heard as an echo.

Tiny bones carry vibrations

Cochlea (fluid filled chamber)

Sound waves vibrate through fluid

Ear drum vibrates

429 Loudspeakers change electrical signals into sounds. The signals in the wire pass through a wire coil inside the speaker. This turns the coil into a magnet, which pushes and pulls against another magnet. The pushing and pulling make the cone vibrate, which sends sound waves into the air.

427 Sound waves spread out from a vibrating object that is moving rapidly to and fro. Stretch an elastic band between your fingers and twang it. As it vibrates, it makes a sound. When you speak, vocal cords in your neck vibrate. You can feel them through your skin.

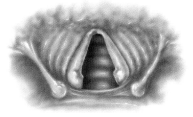

◀ The vocal cords are tough flaps in your voicebox, in your neck.

BOX GUITAR
You will need:

a shoebox   an elastic band
split pins   some card

Cut a hole about 10 centimetres across on one side of an empy shoebox. Push split pins through either side of the hole, and stretch an elastic band between them. Pluck the band. Hear how the air and box vibrate. Cover the hole with card. Is the 'guitar' as loud?

Look out – light's about!

430 Almost everything you do relies on light and the science of light, which is called optics. Light is a form of energy that you can see. Light waves are made of electricity and magnetism – and they are tiny. About 2000 of them laid end to end would stretch across this full stop.

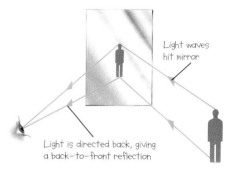

Light waves hit mirror

Light is directed back, giving a back-to-front reflection

▲ Light waves bounce off a mirror.

▼ A prism of clear glass or clear plastic separates the colours in white light.

432 Like sound, light bounces off surfaces which are very smooth. This is called reflection. A mirror is smooth, hard and flat. When you look at it, you see your reflection.

431 Ordinary light from the Sun or from a light bulb is called white light. But when white light passes through a prism, a triangular block of clear glass, it splits into seven colours. These colours are known as the spectrum. Each colour has a different length of wave. A rainbow is made by raindrops which work like millions of tiny prisms to split up sunlight.

433 Light passes through certain materials, like clear glass and plastic. Materials which let light pass through, to give a clear view, are transparent. Those which do not allow light through, like wood and metal, are opaque.

▶ Glass and water bend, or refract, light waves. This makes a drinking straw look bent where it goes behind the glass and then into the water.

434 Mirrors and lenses are important parts of many optical (light-using) gadgets. They are found in cameras, binoculars, microscopes, telescopes and lasers. Without them, we would have no close-up photographs of tiny microchips or insects or giant planets – in fact, no photos at all.

435 Light does not usually go straight through glass. It bends slightly where it goes into the glass, then bends back as it comes out. This is called refraction. A lens is a curved piece of glass or plastic that bends light to make things look bigger, smaller or clearer. Spectacle and contact lenses bend light to help people see more clearly.

▼ A concave lens, which is thin in the middle, makes things look smaller.

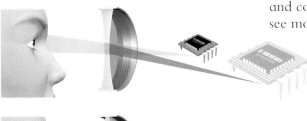

▲ A convex lens, which bulges in the middle, makes things look larger.

I DON'T BELIEVE IT!
Light is the fastest thing in the Universe. It travels through space at 300,000 kilometres per second. That's seven times around the world in less than one second!

The power of lasers

436 Laser light is a special kind of light. Like ordinary light, it is made of waves, but there are three main differences. First, ordinary white light is a mixture of colours. Laser light is just one pure colour. Second, ordinary light waves have peaks (highs) and troughs (lows), which do not line up with each other – laser light waves line up perfectly. Third, an ordinary light beam spreads and fades. A laser beam does not. It can travel for thousands of kilometres as a strong, straight beam.

437 To make a laser beam, energy is fed in short bursts into a substance called the active medium. The energy might be electricity, heat or ordinary light. In a red ruby laser, the active medium is a rod of ruby crystal. A strong lamp makes the tiny particles in the crystal vibrate. They give off energy, which bounces to and fro inside the crystal, off the mirrors at each end. Eventually, the rays vibrate with each other and they are all the same length. The energy becomes so strong that it bursts through a mirror at the end of the crystal.

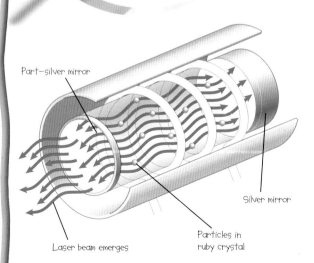

Part–silver mirror

Silver mirror

Laser beam emerges

Particles in ruby crystal

◄ Waves of light build up and bounce to and fro inside a laser, then emerge at one end.

438 Lasers were invented in 1960.

They are used to play CDs and DVDs for music and movies, and in computers. They cut through thick metal in factories, and carry out delicate eye operations. They carry phone calls and television programmes along cables. They even measure movements of the Earth to warn of volcanoes or earthquakes.

▼ An industrial laser has the power to melt metal into gas and cut a neat line.

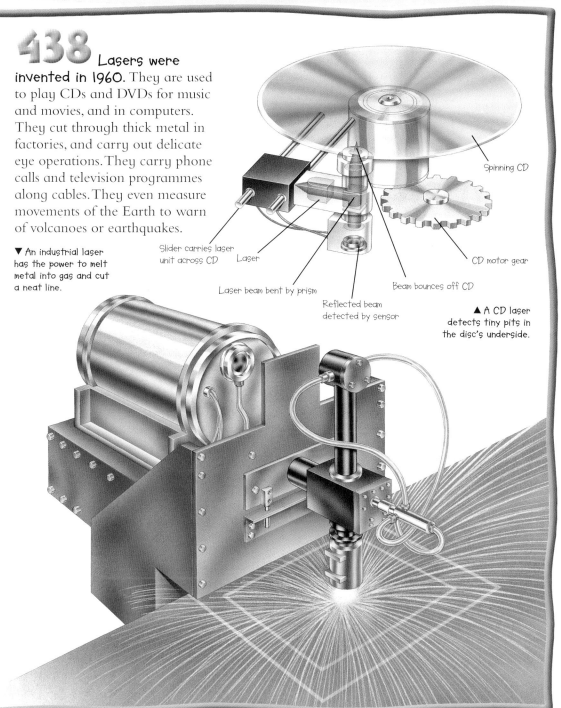

Spinning CD

Slider carries laser unit across CD

Laser

Laser beam bent by prism

Reflected beam detected by sensor

Beam bounces off CD

CD motor gear

▲ A CD laser detects tiny pits in the disc's underside.

Mystery magnets

439 **Without magnets there would be no electric motors, computers or loudspeakers.** Magnetism is an invisible force to do with atoms – tiny particles that make up everything. Atoms are made of even smaller particles, including electrons. Magnetism is linked to the way that these line up and move. Most magnetic substances contain iron. As iron makes up a big part of the metallic substance steel, steel is also magnetic.

440 **A magnet is a lump of iron or steel which has all its electrons and atoms lined up.** This means that their magnetic forces all add up. The force surrounds the magnet, in a region called the magnetic field. This is strongest at the two parts of the magnet called the poles. In a bar or horseshoe magnet, the poles are at the ends.

▶ An electromagnet attracts the body of a car, which is made of iron-based steel.

▼ The field around a magnet affects objects which contain iron.

Magnetic lines of force

Magnetic field

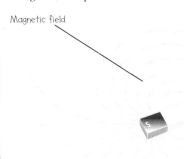

441 **When electricity flows through a wire, it makes a weak magnetic field around it.** If the wire is wrapped into a coil, the magnetism becomes stronger. This is called an electromagnet. Its magnetic force is the same as an ordinary magnet, but when the electricity goes off, the magnetism does too. Some electromagnets are so strong, they can lift whole cars.

442 **A magnet has two different poles – north and south.** A north pole repels (pushes away) the north pole of another magnet. Two south poles also repel each other. But a north pole and a south pole attract (pull together). Both magnetic poles attract any substance containing iron, like a nail or a screw.

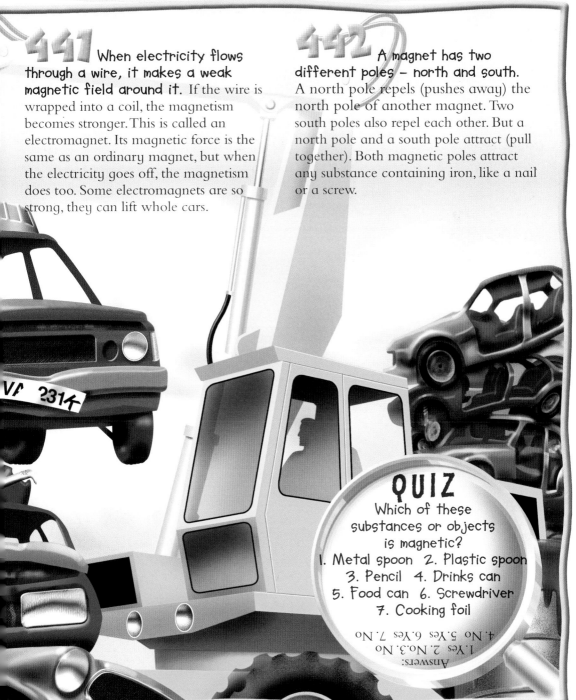

VA 2314

QUIZ
Which of these substances or objects is magnetic?
1. Metal spoon 2. Plastic spoon
3. Pencil 4. Drinks can
5. Food can 6. Screwdriver
7. Cooking foil

Answers:
1.Yes 2.No 3.No 4.No 5.Yes 6.Yes 7.No

Electric sparks!

443 **Flick the switch and things happen.** The television goes off, the computer comes on, lights shine and music plays. Electricity is our favourite form of energy. We send it along wires and plug hundreds of machines into it. Imagine no washing machine, no electric light and no vacuum cleaner!

▶ Electricity is bits of atoms moving along a wire.

Atom

Electron

444 **Electricity depends on electrons, tiny parts of atoms.** In certain substances, when electrons are 'pushed', they hop from one atom to the next. When billions do this every second, electricity flows. The 'push' is from a battery or the generator at a power station. Electricity only flows if it can go in a complete loop or circuit. Break the circuit and the flow stops.

445 **A battery makes electricity from chemicals.** Two different chemicals next to each other, such as an acid and a metal, swap electrons and get the flow going. Electricity's pushing strength is measured in volts. Most batteries are 1.5, 3, 6 or 9 volts, with 12 volts in cars.

446 **Electricity flows easily through some substances, including water and metals.** These are electrical conductors. Other substances do not allow electricity to flow. They are insulators. Insulators include wood, plastic, glass, card and ceramics. Metal wires and cables have coverings of plastic, to stop the electricity leaking away.

Positive contact

◀ A battery has a chemical paste inside a metal casing.

Negative contact on bo

447 Electricity from power stations is carried along cables on high pylons, or buried underground. This is known as the distribution grid. At thousands of volts, this electricity is very dangerous. For use in the home, it is changed to 220 volts (in Britain). But it can still easily kill a person.

▼ A power station makes enough electricity for thousands of homes.

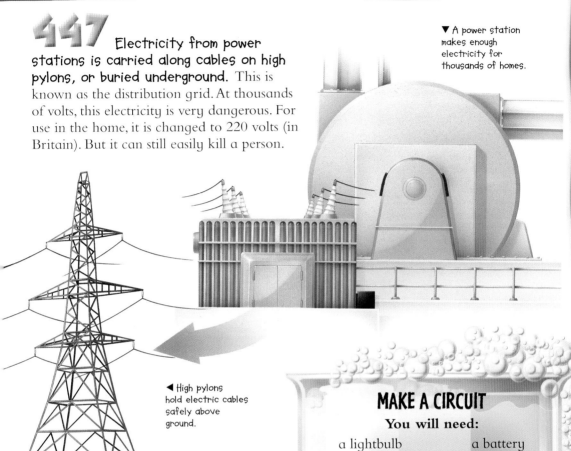

◄ High pylons hold electric cables safely above ground.

448 Mains electricity is made at a power station. A fuel such as coal or oil is burned to heat water into high-pressure steam. The steam pushes past the blades of a turbine and makes them spin. The spinning motion turns coils of wire near powerful magnets, and this makes electricity flow in the coils.

MAKE A CIRCUIT
You will need:

a lightbulb	a battery
some wire	a plastic ruler
a metal spoon	some dry card

Join a bulb to a battery with pieces of wire, as shown. Electricity flows round the circuit and lights the bulb. Make a gap in the circuit and put various objects into it, to see if they allow electricity to flow again. Try a plastic ruler, a metal spoon and some dry card.

Making sounds and pictures

449 The air is full of waves we cannot see or hear, unless we have the right machine. Radio waves are a form of electrical and magnetic energy, just like heat and light waves, microwaves and X-rays. All of these are called electromagnetic waves and they travel at an equal speed – the speed of light.

450 Radio waves are used for both radio and television. They travel vast distances. Long waves curve around the Earth's surface. Short waves bounce between the Earth and the sky.

▼ All these waves are the same form of energy. They all differ in length.

▲ A radio set picks up radio waves using its long aerial or antenna.

451 Radio waves carry their information by being altered, or modulated, in a certain pattern. The height of a wave is called its amplitude. If this is altered, it is known as AM (amplitude modulation). Look for AM on the radio display.

452 The number of waves per second is called the frequency. If this is altered, it is known as FM (frequency modulation). FM radio is clearer than AM, and less affected by weather and thunderstorms.

| Long radio waves | Shorter radio waves (TV) | Microwaves | Light waves | X-rays | Short X-rays | Gamma rays |

453

Radio and TV programmes may be sent out as radio waves from a tall tower on the ground. The tower is called a transmitter. Sometimes waves may be broadcast (sent) by a satellite in space. Or the programmes may not even arrive as radio waves. They can come as flashes of laser light, as cable TV and radio.

▶ A dish-shaped receiver picks up radio waves for TV channels.

454

Inside a TV set, the pattern of radio waves is changed into electrical signals. Some go to the loudspeaker to make the sounds. Others go to the screen to make the pictures. Inside most televisions, the screen is at the front of a glass container called a tube. At the back of the tube are electron guns. These fire streams of electrons. The inside of the screen is coated with thousands of tiny coloured dots called phosphors. When electrons hit the dots, they glow and make the picture.

▼ A TV screen's three colours of patches or dots combine to make up the other colours.

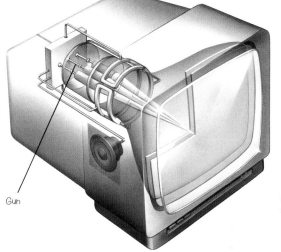

Gun

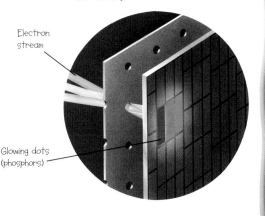

Electron stream

Glowing dots (phosphors)

Compu-science

455 **Computers are amazing machines.** But they have to be told exactly what to do. So we put in instructions and information, by various means. These include typing on a keyboard, inserting a disc, using a joystick or games board, or linking up a camera, scanner or another computer.

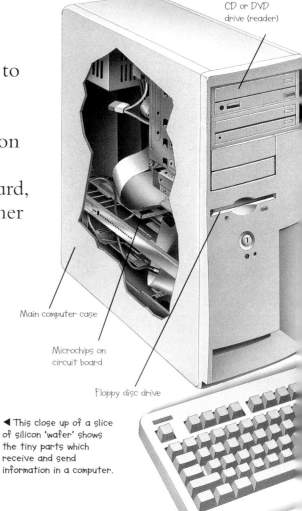

CD or DVD drive (reader)

Main computer case

Microchips on circuit board

Floppy disc drive

456 **Most computers are controlled by instructions from a keyboard and a mouse.** The mouse moves a pointer around on the screen and its click buttons select choices from lists called menus.

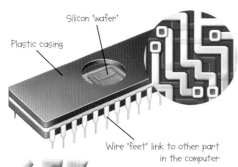

Silicon 'wafer'

Plastic casing

Wire 'feet' link to other part in the computer

◀ This close up of a slice of silicon 'wafer' shows the tiny parts which receive and send information in a computer.

457 **Some computers are controlled by talking to them!** They pick up the sounds using a microphone. This is VR, or voice recognition technology.

458 **The 'brain' of a computer is its Central Processing Unit.** It is usually a microchip – millions of electronic parts on a chip of silicon, hardly larger than a fingernail. It receives information and instructions from other microchips, carries out the work, and sends back the results.

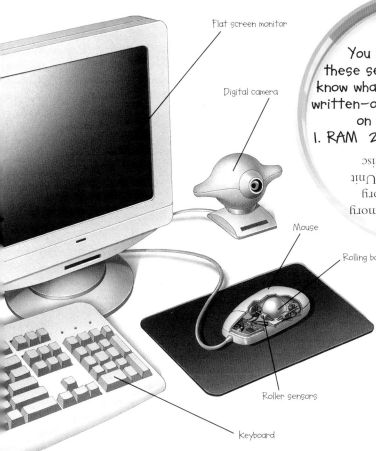

Flat screen monitor

Digital camera

Mouse

Rolling ball

Roller sensors

Keyboard

QUIZ

You may have heard of these sets of letters. Do you know what they mean? Their full written-out versions are all here on these two pages.
1. RAM 2. ROM 3. CPU 4. DVD

Answers:
1. Random Access Memory
2. Read Only Memory
3. Central Processing Unit
4. Digital Versatile Disc

◄ This is a PC, or personal computer. The keyboard is like a typewriter, but has extra keys called function keys. These make the computer do certain tasks. By using the mouse to move a pointer (cursor) around the screen, certain instructions can be clicked on. This can be quicker than using the keyboard.

460 Once the computer has done its task, it feeds out the results. These usually go to a screen called a monitor, where we see them. But they can also go to a printer, a loudspeaker or even a robot arm. Or they can be stored on a disc such as a magnetic disc, compact disc or Digital Versatile Disc (DVD).

459 Information and instructions are contained in the computer in memory microchips. There are two kinds. Random Access Memory is like a jotting pad. It keeps changing as the computer carries out its tasks. Read Only Memory is like an instruction book. It usually contains the instructions for how the computer starts up and how all the microchips work together.

Web around the world

461 **The world is at your fingertips – if you are on the Internet.** The 'Net' is one of the most amazing results of modern-day science. It is a worldwide network of computers, linked like one huge electrical spider's web.

A modem changes telephone signals to computer signals

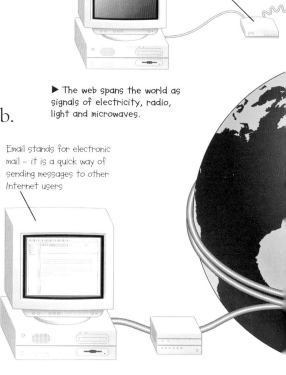

▶ The web spans the world as signals of electricity, radio, light and microwaves.

Email stands for electronic mail – it is a quick way of sending messages to other Internet users

▲ As mobile phones get smaller, they can also connect to the Net using their radio link.

462 **Signals travel from computer to computer in many ways.** These include electricity along telephone wires, flashes of laser light along fibre-optic cables or radio waves between tall towers. Information is changed from one form to another in a split second. It can also travel between computers on different sides of the world in less than a second using satellite links.

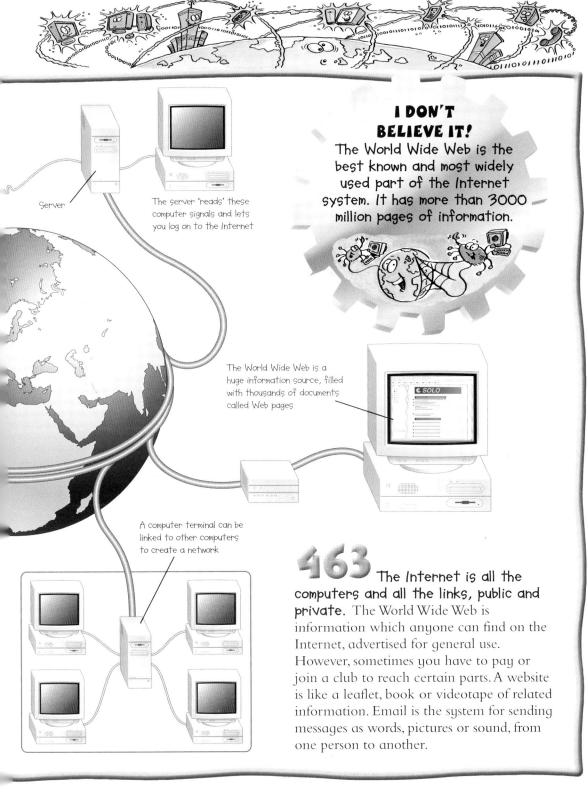

Server

The server 'reads' these computer signals and lets you log on to the Internet

The World Wide Web is a huge information source, filled with thousands of documents called Web pages

€ SOLO

A computer terminal can be linked to other computers to create a network

463 The Internet is all the computers and all the links, public and private. The World Wide Web is information which anyone can find on the Internet, advertised for general use. However, sometimes you have to pay or join a club to reach certain parts. A website is like a leaflet, book or videotape of related information. Email is the system for sending messages as words, pictures or sound, from one person to another.

What's it made of?

464 You would not make a bridge out of straw, or a cup out of thin paper! Choosing the right substance or material for a job is part of materials science. All the substances in the world can be divided into several groups. The biggest group is metals such as iron, copper, silver, and gold. Most metals are strong, hard and shiny, and carry heat and electricity well. They are used where materials must be tough and long-lasting.

465 Plastics are made mainly from the substances in petroleum (crude oil). There are so many kinds – some are hard and brittle while others are soft and bendy. They are usually long-lasting, not affected by weather or damp, and they resist heat and electricity.

▼ A racing car has thousands of parts made from hundreds of materials. Each is suited to certain conditions such as stress, temperature and vibrations.

Each tyre is made of thick, tough rubber to withstand high speeds

The front wing is a special shape – this produces a force that presses the car down onto the track

The main body of the car is made from carbon fibre, a light but very strong material

The car's axles are made from titanium – a very strong, light metal

466 Ceramics are materials based on clay or other substances dug from the Earth. They can be shaped and dried, like a clay bowl. Or they can be fired – baked in a hot oven called a kiln. This makes them hard and long-lasting, but brittle and prone to cracks. Ceramics resist heat and electricity very well.

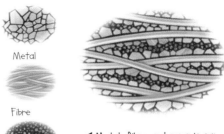

Metal

Fibre

Ceramic

◀ Metal, fibre and ceramic can combine to make a composite material (above). The way all of these ingredients are arranged can affect the composite's strength.

467 Glass is produced from the raw substances limestone and sand. When heated at a high temperature, these become a clear, gooey liquid, which sets hard as it cools. Its great advantage is that you can see through it.

468 Composites are mixtures or combinations of different materials. For example, glass strands are coated with plastic to make GRP – glass-reinforced plastic. This composite has the advantages of both materials.

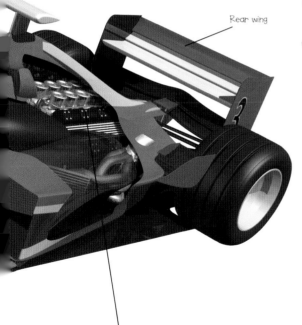

Rear wing

The engine can produce about 10 times as much power as an ordinary car – but it needs to be as light as possible

MAKE YOUR OWN COMPOSITE
You will need:

flour   newspaper strips

water   balloon   pin

You can make a composite called pâpier maché from flour, newspaper and water.

Tear newspaper into strips. Mix flour and water into a paste. Dip each strip in the paste and place it around a blown-up balloon. Cover the balloon and allow it to dry. Pop the balloon with a pin, and the composite should stay in shape.

The world of chemicals

469 **The world is made of chemical substances.** Some are completely pure. Others are mixtures of substances – such as petroleum (crude oil). Petroleum provides us with thousands of different chemicals and materials, such as plastics, paints, soaps and fuel. It is one of the most useful, and valuable, substances in the world.

Fumes and vapours condense into liquid

▶ The huge tower (fractionating column) of an oil refinery may be 50 metres high.

470 **In an oil refinery, crude oil is heated in a huge tower.** Some of its different substances turn into fumes (vapours) and rise up the tower. The fumes turn back into liquids at different heights inside the tower, due to the different temperatures at each level. We get petrol in this way. Remaining at the bottom of the tower are thick, gooey tars, asphalts and bitumens – which are used to make road surfaces.

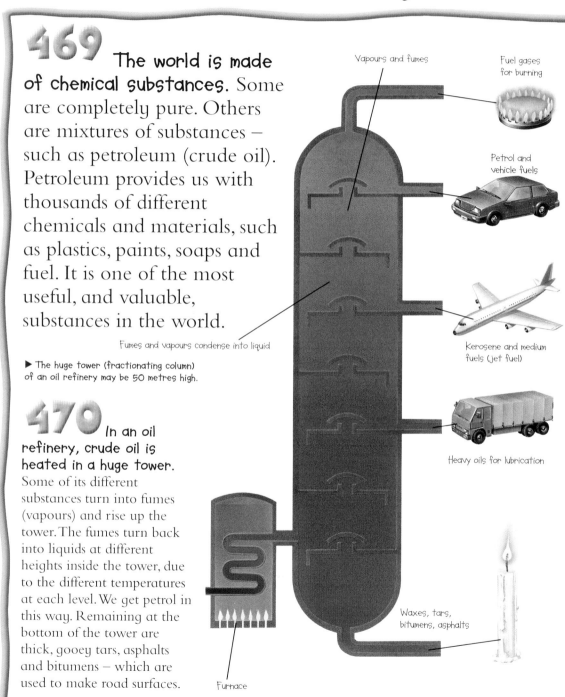

Vapours and fumes

Fuel gases for burning

Petrol and vehicle fuels

Kerosene and medium fuels (jet fuel)

Heavy oils for lubrication

Waxes, tars, bitumens, asphalts

Furnace

471 **One group of chemicals is called acids.** They vary in strength from very weak citric acid which gives the sharp taste to fruits such as lemons, to extremely strong and dangerous sulphuric acid in a car battery. Powerful acids burn and corrode, or eat away, substances. Some even corrode glass or steel.

472 **Another group of chemicals is bases.** They vary in strength from weak alkaloids, which give the bitter taste to coffee beans, to strong bases in drain cleaners and industrial polishes. Bases feel soapy or slimy and, like acids, they can burn or corrode.

▼ Indicator paper changes colour when it touches different substances. Acids turn it red, alkalis make it bluish-purple. The deeper the colour, the stronger the acid or base.

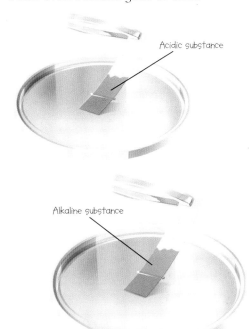

Acidic substance

Alkaline substance

Neutral substance

473 **Acids and bases are 'opposite' types of chemicals.** When they meet, they undergo changes called chemical reactions. The result is usually a third chemical, called a salt. The common salt we use for cooking is one example. Its chemical name is sodium chloride.

FROTHY FUN
You will need:
some vinegar   washing soda

Create a chemical reaction by adding a few drops of vinegar to a spoonful of washing soda in a saucer. The vinegar is an acid, the soda is a base. The two react by frothing and giving off bubbles of carbon dioxide gas. What is left is a salt (but not to be eaten).

Pure science

474 The world seems to be made of millions of different substances – such as soil, wood, concrete, plastics and air. These are combinations of simpler substances. If you could take them apart, you would see that they are made of pure substances called elements.

H Hydrogen 1										
Li Lithium 3	Be Beryllium 4									
Na Sodium 11	Mg Magnesium 12									

K Potassium 19	Ca Calcium 20	Sc Scandium 21	Ti Titanium 22	V Vanadium 23	Cr Chromium 24	Mn Manganese 25	Fe Iron 26	Co Cobalt 27	Ni Nickel 28	Cu Copper 29	Zn Zinc 30
Rb Rubidium 37	Sr Strontium 38	Y Yttrium 39	Zr Zirconium 40	Nb Niobium 41	Mo Molybdenum 42	Tc Technetium 43	Ru Ruthenium 44	Rh Rhodium 45	Pd Palladium 46	Ag Silver 47	Cd Cadmium 48
Cs Caesium 55	Ba Barium 56		Hf Hafnium 72	Ta Tantalum 73	W Tungsten 74	Re Rhenium 75	Os Osmium 76	Ir Iridium 77	Pt Platinum 78	Au Gold 79	Hg Mercury 80
Fr Francium 87	Ra Radium 88		Rf Rutherfordium 104	Db Dubnium 105	Sg Seaborgium 106	Bh Bohrium 107	Hs Hassium 108	Mt Meitnerium 109	Uun Ununnilium 110	Uuu Unununium 111	Uub Ununbium 112
			La Lanthanum 57	Ce Cerium 58	Pr Praseodymium 59	Nd Neodymium 60	Pm Promethium 61	Sm Samarium 62	Eu Europium 63	Gd Gadolinium 64	Tb Terbium 65
			Ac Actinium 89	Th Thorium 90	Pa Protactinium 91	U Uranium 92	Np Neptunium 93	Pu Plutonium 94	Am Americium 95	Cm Curium 96	Bk Berkelium 97

475 Hydrogen is the simplest element. This means it has the smallest atoms. It is a very light gas, which floats upwards in air. Hydrogen was once used to fill giant airships. But there was a problem – hydrogen catches fire easily and explodes. In fact, stars are made mainly of burning hydrogen, which is why they are so hot and bright.

476 About 90 elements are found naturally on and in the Earth. In an element, all of its particles, called atoms, are exactly the same as each other. Just as important, they are all different from the atoms of any other element.

▼ The elements can be arranged in a table. Each has a letter, like C for carbon. It also has a number showing how big or heavy its atoms are compared to those of other elements.

					He Helium 2
B Boron 5	C Carbon 6	N Nitrogen 7	O Oxygen 8	F Flourine 9	Ne Neon 10
Al Aluminium 13	Si Silicon 14	P Phosphorus 15	S Sulphur 16	Cl Chlorine 17	Ar Argon 18
Ga Gallium 31	Ge Germanium 32	As Arsenic 33	Se Selenium 34	Br Bromine 35	Kr Krypton 36
In Indium 49	Sn Tin 50	Sb Antimony 51	Te Tellurium 52	I Iodine 53	Xe Xenon 54
Tl Thalium 81	Pb Lead 82	Bi Bismuth 83	Po Polonium 84	At Astatine 85	Rn Radon 86

Dy Dysprosium 66	Ho Holmium 67	Er Erbium 68	Tm Thulium 69	Yb Ytterbium 70	Lu Lutetium 71
Cf Californium 98	Es Einsteinium 99	Fm Fermium 100	Md Mendelevium 101	No Nobelium 102	Lr Lawrencium 103

QUIZ

1. Where does petrol come from?
2. What usually happens when you mix an acid and a base?
3. Which element makes up stars?
4. What do diamonds and coal have in common?

Answers:
1. Petroleum 2. They react to form a salt 3. Hydrogen 4. They are both made of pure carbon

478 Uranium is a heavy and dangerous element. It gives off harmful rays and tiny particles, called radioactivity. These can cause sickness, burns and diseases such as cancer. Radioactivity is a type of energy and, under careful control, it may be used as fuel in nuclear power stations.

479 Aluminium is an element which is a metal, and it is one of the most useful in modern life. It is light and strong, it does not rust, and it is resistant to corrosion. Saucepans, drinks cans, cooking foil and jet planes are made mainly of aluminium.

477 Carbon is a very important element in living things – including our own bodies. It joins easily with atoms of other elements to make large groups of atoms called molecules. When it is pure, carbon can be two different forms. These are soft, powdery soot, and hard, glittering diamond. The form depends on how the carbon atoms join to each other.

▶ Carbon can be hard diamond or soft soot, which is made of sheets of joined atoms.

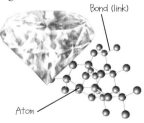

Bond (link)

Atom

Small science

480 **Many pages in this book mention atoms.** They are the smallest bits of a substance. They are so tiny, even a billion atoms would be too small to see. But scientists have carried out experiments to find out what's inside an atom. The answer is – even smaller bits. These are sub-atomic particles, and there are three main kinds.

481 **At the centre of each atom is a blob called the nucleus.** It contains an equal number of two kinds of sub-atomic particles. These are protons and neutrons. The proton is like the north pole of a magnet. It is positive, or plus. The neutron is not. It is neither positive or negative.

I DON'T BELIEVE IT!
One hundred years ago, people thought the electrons were spread out in an atom, like the raisins in a raisin pudding.

Electron

Ball-shaped shells which contain electrons

Nucleus

482 Atoms of the various elements have different numbers of protons and neutrons. An atom of hydrogen has just one proton. An atom of helium, the gas put in party balloons to make them float, has one proton and one neutron. An atom of the heavy metal called lead has 82 protons and neutrons.

▶ The bits inside an atom give each substance its features, from exploding hydrogen to life-giving oxygen.

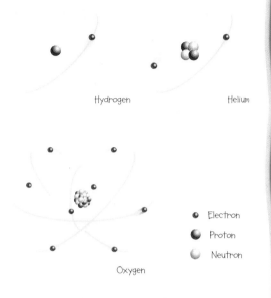

Hydrogen

Helium

Oxygen

● Electron

● Proton

● Neutron

Movement of electrons

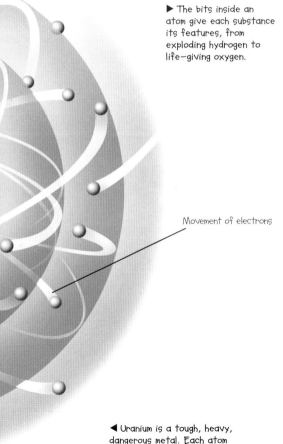

◀ Uranium is a tough, heavy, dangerous metal. Each atom of uranium has 92 electrons whizzing around its nucleus.

483 Around the centre of each atom are sub-atomic particles called electrons. They whizz round and round the nucleus. In the same way that a proton in the nucleus is positive or plus, an electron is negative or minus. The number of protons and neutrons is usually the same, so the plus and minus numbers are the same. (Electrons are the bits which jump from atom to atom when electricity flows).

484 It is hard to imagine that atoms are so small. A grain of sand, smaller than this o, contains at least 100 billion billion atoms. If you could make the atoms bigger, so that each one becomes as big as a pin head, the grain of sand would be two kilometres high!

Scientists at work

485 **There are thousands of different jobs and careers in science.** Scientists work in laboratories, factories, offices, mines, steelworks, nature parks and almost everywhere else. They find new knowledge and make discoveries using a process called the scientific method.

486 **First comes an idea, called a theory or hypothesis.** This asks or predicts what will happen in a certain situation. Scientists continually come up with new ideas and theories to test. One very simple theory is – if I throw a ball up in the air, will it come back down?

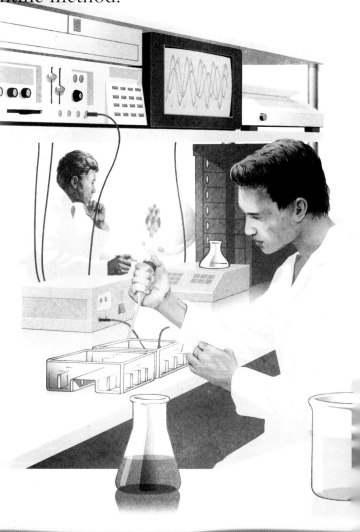

487 **The scientist carries out an experiment or test, to check what happens.** The experiment is carefully designed and controlled, so that it will reveal useful results. Any changes are carried out one at a time, so that the effect of each change can be studied. The experiment for our simple theory is – throw the ball up in the air.

488 Measuring and recording are very important as part of the experiment. All the changes are measured, written down, and perhaps photographed or filmed as well.

▼ Scientists carrying out research in a laboratory gather information and record all of their findings.

489 The results are what happens during and at the end of the experiment. They are studied, perhaps by drawing graphs and making tables. You can probably guess the result of our experiment – the ball falls back down.

490 At the end of this scientific process, the scientist thinks of reasons or conclusions about why certain things happened. The conclusion for our experiment is – something pulls the ball back down. But science never stands still. There are always new theories, experiments and results. This is how science progresses, with more discoveries and inventions every year.

QUIZ

Put these activities in the correct order, so that a scientist can carry out the scientific method.
1. Results 2. Experiment
3. Conclusions 4. Theory
5. Measurements

Answer:
4, 2, 5, 1, 3

Science in nature

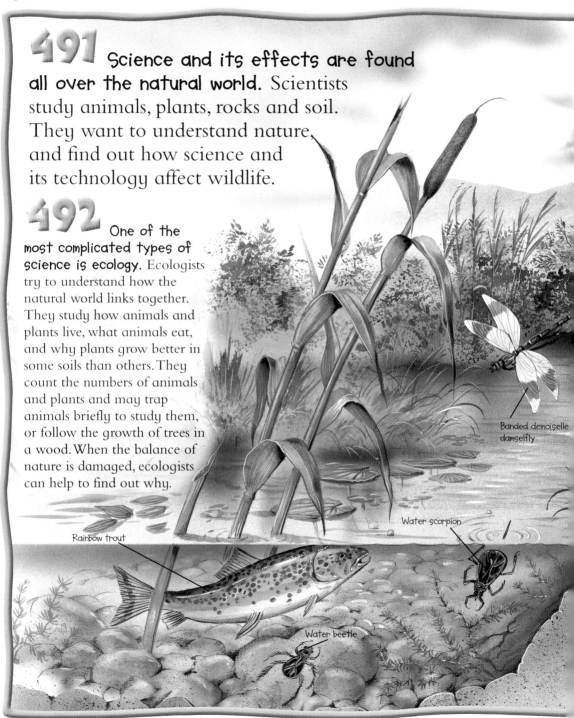

491 **Science and its effects are found all over the natural world.** Scientists study animals, plants, rocks and soil. They want to understand nature, and find out how science and its technology affect wildlife.

492 **One of the most complicated types of science is ecology.** Ecologists try to understand how the natural world links together. They study how animals and plants live, what animals eat, and why plants grow better in some soils than others. They count the numbers of animals and plants and may trap animals briefly to study them, or follow the growth of trees in a wood. When the balance of nature is damaged, ecologists can help to find out why.

Banded demoiselle damselfly

Water scorpion

Rainbow trout

Water beetle

One of the most important jobs in science is to study damage and pollution in the natural world. Almost everything we make or do affects wild places with their animals and plants. Factories, power stations and roadways crammed with vehicles are especially harmful, as chemicals spread in the air and seep into soil and water.

Reedmace

Power station

Heron

Otter

Warbler

493 Ecologists use many forms of high-tech science in their studies. They may fit an animal with a radio-collar so that its movements can be tracked. Special cameras see in the dark and show how night hunters catch their prey. Radar used to detect planes can also follow flocks of birds. The sonar (echo-sounding) equipment of boats can track shoals of fish or whales.

I DON'T BELIEVE IT!
Science explains how animals such as birds or whales find their way across the world. Some detect the Earth's magnetism, and which way is north or south. Others follow changes in gravity, the force which pulls everything to the Earth's surface.

Body science

494 One of the biggest areas of science is medicine. Medical scientists work to produce better drugs, more spare parts for the body and more machines for use by doctors. They also carry out scientific research to find out how people can stay healthy and prevent disease.

▼ As a runner gets tired, his heart pumps harder. Its beats can be detected and shown on an ECG machine.

ECG machine showing display

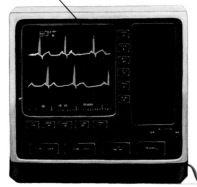

Sensor pad

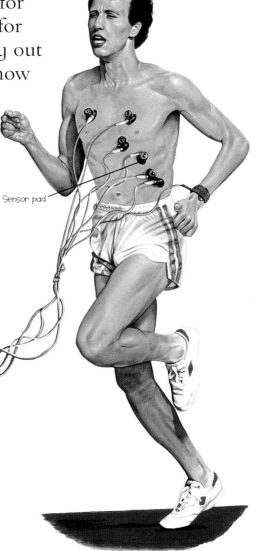

495 As parts of the body work, such as the muscles and nerves, they produce tiny pulses of electricity. Pads on the skin pick up these pulses, which are displayed as a wavy line on a screen or paper strip. The ECG (electro-cardiograph) machine shows the heart beating. The EEG (electro-encephalograph) shows nerve signals flashing around the brain.

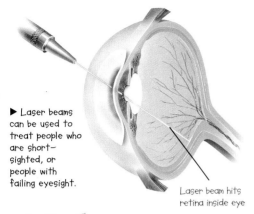

▶ Laser beams can be used to treat people who are short-sighted, or people with failing eyesight.

Laser beam hits retina inside eye

496

Laser beams are ideal for delicate operations, or surgery, on body parts such as the eye. The beam makes very small, precise cuts. It can be shone into the eye and made most focused, or strongest, inside. So it can make a cut deep within the eye, without any harm to the outer parts.

▼ An endoscope is inserted into the body to give a doctor a picture on screen. The treatment can be given immediately.

497

The endoscope is like a flexible telescope made of fibre-optic strands. This is pushed into a body opening such as the mouth, or through a small cut, to see inside. The surgeon looks into the other end of the endoscope, or at a picture on a screen.

Endoscope tube

Image from endoscope

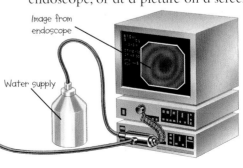

Water supply

Science in the future

498 **Many modern machines and processes can cause damage to our environment and our health.** The damage includes acid rain, destruction of the ozone layer and the greenhouse effect, leading to climate change and global warming. Science can help to find solutions. New filters and chemicals called catalysts can reduce dangerous fumes from vehicle exhausts and power stations, and in the chemicals in factory waste pipes.

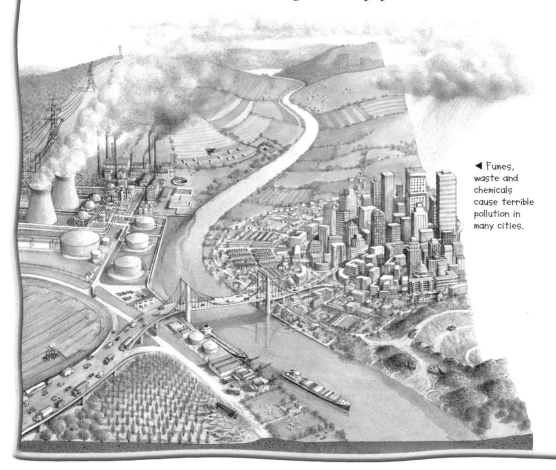

◀ Fumes, waste and chemicals cause terrible pollution in many cities.

499 One very important area of science is recycling. Many materials and substances can be recycled – glass, paper, plastics, cans, scrap metals and rags. Scientists are working to improve the process. Products should be designed so that when they no longer work, they are easy to recycle. The recycling process itself is also being made more effective.

Bottle crusher

Bottle bank

▼ Recycling glass saves enormous amounts of energy and raw materials.

Moulds

QUIZ

If you become a scientist, which science would you like to study? See if you can guess what these sciences are:
1. Meteorology 2. Biology
3. Astronomy 4. Ecology

Answers:
1. Weather and climate
2. Animals, plants and other living things 3. Stars, planets and objects in space 4. The way nature works

500 We use vast amounts of energy, especially to make electricity and as fuel in our cars. Much of this energy comes from crude oil (petroleum), natural gas and coal. But these energy sources will not last for ever. They also cause huge amounts of pollution. Scientists are working to develop cleaner forms of energy, which will produce less pollution and not run out. These include wind power from turbines, solar power from photocells, and hydroelectric and tidal power from dams.

▼ The energy in flowing water can be turned into electricity at a hydroelectric power station.

Let's have some fun!

WORD SCRAMBLE

Unscramble the letters to find the names of the world's oceans.

1. CTRAIC 2. CIFAPCI
3. NALATCIT 4. ANDINI

Answers:
1. Arctic 2. Pacific
3. Atlantic 4. Indian

ODD ONE OUT

Which of these planets is the odd one out?

1. Mars
2. Jupiter
3. Saturn
4. Neptune

Answer:
1. Mars – it is a rocky planet,
the others are gas planets

WORD SEARCH

Can you find the names of the four seasons hidden in this grid?

S	P	R	I	N	G	Q	A
M	Z	U	A	N	L	U	W
U	R	L	D	N	T	V	I
M	R	L	E	U	N	B	N
Y	T	V	M	A	A	E	T
K	A	N	D	J	W	Z	E
R	E	M	M	U	S	H	R

QUIZ

You may have heard of these sets of letters. Do you know what they mean?

1. WWW 2. ROM
3. CPU 4. CD

Answers:
1. World Wide Web
2. Read Only Memory
3. Central Processing Unit
4. Compact Disc

Can you remember?

Look at the picture above. Name the different satellites and say what they are used for.
Look at the picture below. How many different forms of transport can you see?

Index